to: Dr. Sayed Nour
with my great admiration

Nasr Arif
Dubai, 8-10-2000

WESTERN POLITICAL SCIENCE IN A NON-WESTERN CONTEXT

Theories of Comparative Politics in the Arab Academia

Nasr M. Arif

University Press of America, Inc.
Lanham · New York · Oxford

Copyright © 2001 by
University Press of America,® Inc.
4720 Boston Way
Lanham, Maryland 20706

12 Hid's Copse Rd.
Cumnor Hill, Oxford OX2 9JJ

Library of Congress Cataloging-in-Publication Data

Arif, Nasr Muhammad
Western political science in a non-western context : theories of
comparative politics in the Arab academia / Nasr M. Arif.
p.   cm
Includes bibliographical references and index.
1. Political science—Arab countries. 2. Arab countries—Politics
and government. 3. Comparative government. I. Title.
JA84.A6 A75   2000   320.3'0917'4927—dc21   00-048816 CIP

ISBN 0-7618-1840-5 (cloth: alk. ppr.)

Contents

Introduction   v

Chapter I: Comparative Methodology in Arabic Literature:
The State of the Discipline   1

Chapter II: Attempts to Adapt and Develop Theoretical
Frameworks to Study Arab Political Systems   23

Chapter III: Reconstructing a Theoretical Approach for the Study
of Arab Political Systems: Epistemological Foundations   39

Chapter IV: Elite Approach as a Model for Theory Adaptation
to Study Arab Political Systems: Potential and Problematic   55

Chapter V: A Linguistic Approach to the Arab Politics:
The Epistemological Connotation of the Arab Reconciliation   71

Conclusion   93

Bibliography   95

Index   103

Introduction

Physical sciences deal with issues that are either true or false. Experiments are conducted to discover the precise laws that control the universal physical domain. When it comes to the issues of social science, however, it has been customary not to bother with whether theories are valid or not—it is more rewarding to examine and describe the context in which the issues occur, for they are directly and inextricably intertwined with their specific social, local, and temporal environments[1] Social sciences are hermeneutical, i.e., they are based on understanding interlocking phenomenon rather than explaining cause and effect. Therefore, definition of the extent to which bias exists has to begin with a clear and careful differentiation between the concepts of accuracy and validity. Socio-political notions and theories may be accurate in themselves and valid in a particular environment, yet they can be inoperative in another. What is at issue is not their internal logical accuracy but their validity—or capability of understanding what sort of change will lead to improvement for the better in a given society. At this juncture, bias in social sciences is conceived of as an attempt to force a reconciliation between accuracy and validity. In other words, bias exists when a social scientist generalizes and universalizes theories and ideas out of their own socio-cultural sphere just because they were accurate and valid in that particular societal context.

In the social sciences, the phenomena that we study are not material ones. We are limited to investigating them indirectly rather than directly. Researchers deal with these phenomena by using mediators such as concepts, methodologies, and theories that serve to transmit events from actual reality to the human mind—which then attempts to understand, analyze, and explain them. The extent to which man can understand reality is dependent upon the tools he uses in the process of transmitting information from reality to the abstract. We can only understand social phenomena with a degree of accuracy that parallels the analytical and explanatory range of the tools being used. Research tools are not neutral because they provide a framework for selectively deducing those elements that conform with the structure of the tools themselves. They do not reflect the society as it actually is. They are value-laden and form one part of a triad whose two other components are the "mind" and the "social reality."

Hence, even those concepts, methodologies, and theories that appear to be quite comprehensive and accurate can only investigate certain dimensions, not all, of social reality. It is obvious that it is not possible to investigate all of the components or details of a given society. Only certain dimensions of that reality are selected—those that are judged to be the most significant in abstracting key elements of the reality, leading to a substantial understanding and accurate analysis of it. Some theories or methodologies rely on class as an approach to understanding and explaining social and political phenomena. Others focus on elites, groups, structures, functions, or decision-making, etc. In spite of their differing emphases, all of these theories and methodologies are based on accepting the assumption that not all dimensions of the phenomenon can be identified, studied, and understood. One possibility for minimizing this unavoidable process of reduction, however, is to identify a specific dimension as the subject of intense focus on the basis of its being regarded as the axial dimension of the society. This approach implies that the identification and investigation of the axial dimension is important to attaining an accurate analysis and full understanding of complex sociological phenomenon.

The researcher needs to be aware of the various theories of his discipline or field of specialization so as to understand the potentialities of each theory, its strengths and weaknesses, its explanatory power, and its limitations. In addition, the researcher must thoroughly understand the most significant characteristics, determinants, and features of the political and social reality within which these phenomena exist. This mode of understanding leads to a clarification of the concept of "methodological co-valence"[2] or "methodological suitability."[3] There should be some sort of covalence, adjusted proportions, and suitability between the phenomena being studied and the theory or methodology applied to approach it. Thus, the methodological tool should "fit" the phenomenon; or, in other words, it should reflect the actual dimensions of the phenomenon in the same proportions that exist in reality, without reducing or altering one or more of these relative weights and proportions. Through this process, the ultimate goal of using the theory or methodology—understanding the reality and explaining it in a way that is closest to accuracy and truth—will be fulfilled. Conversely, a fatal research error occurs when proving the applicability of the theory or methodology becomes a goal in itself.

Taking comparative politics as a case study of the social sciences, we should point out that this field has passed through four stages since the beginning of this century: the first stage which was dominated by historical, legal and institutional theories; the second stage with its main theories focused on class, groups and elites; the third stage in which behaviorism reconstructed the entire field and the systems theories, structural-functional analysis, and decision making approach emerged; and the last stage of post-behaviorism where the main theories employ concepts of dependency, state-society relation, corporatism, political economy, and the new Marxism. This is the evolution of the field of comparative politics in its home society, and yet it has been considered to represent a global episteme. There are a number of questions that arise, however: How has this field been perceived by non-western scientific communities? Have these theories been used in the Arabic literature on comparative politics, and how? What was the position of comparative literature in Arab political writings? What are the most attractive theories? Is there any continuity between the Arab scientific community's progress and developments in comparative politics in the west? Is there a time gap as well as an epistemological one? Is there any attempt to adapt and manipulate these theories to suit the political reality of the Arab region? Have new theories been developed to study Arab political systems? What are the guidelines for real and meticulous work in that area? These are the most important issues that arise in Arab political thought after assimilating the general features of the theoretical structure of comparative politics.

This monograph will investigate these issues in order to present a clearer picture of the field of comparative politics in Arab academic literature. To achieve this goal, the following methodological criteria will guide my analysis:

1. **This study is not going to discuss the degree of relevance of theories of comparative politics developed in the west to the study of Arab political systems.** This deserves a separate study analyzing the relevance of each theory to the Arab political systems. This study aims to understand and analyze how Arab scholars dealt with these theories in the Arab comparative politics literature.
2. **We must assert that the Arab reality is not homogenous—it is rather diverse.** Hence there is no standard model to study a certain Arab polity

in this era. There is plurality and diversity in systems and frameworks, whether political, social, economic, or cultural. This means that internal comparative studies are necessary to arrive at generalizations that can contribute to an understanding of Arab political systems based on reality and not on biased notions projected on reality. Even if there is a singular Arab system that stands in opposition to other holistic systems, that does not imply the absence of plurality within it. In this work I am going to examine studies that are based on this reality and compare between Arab political systems on the basis of an assumption of a diverse Arab reality which does not necessarily negate the possibility of a holistic unity in some aspects.

3. **While these theories are diverse, multiple, and highly adaptable, they can be made understandable through an approach that utilizes epistemological research.** Hence deconstruction and reconstruction will be used to determine the network of relations within the structure of each theory and its component units. This allows us to determine the ideological, epistemological, or societal biases—and proceed to neutralize them in order to reach general frameworks that are applicable in different cultural and social contexts. This also allows for the adaptation and development of these theories in ways that suit Arab social and political phenomena.

4. **Most theories of comparative politics are multifaceted.** They can be perceived as sets of issues within a given episteme, theory and framework for analysis and interpretation, or ideology. Because of the intermingling and development of these aspects in the Arab academic practice, this study will concentrate its emphasis on methodological and theoretical aspects, and not the ideological dimension. When we use the term class analysis, for example, we are not trying to draw a class map of the Arab world, nor do we use class as an ideology based on Marxist beliefs. We are interested in class analysis or class theory as an approach to the study of political phenomena, whether Marxist or not. The same applies to other theories.

Notes

1. Ali Shari'ati, *al-Awoda ila al-dhat*, [rediscovering the core identity] translated from Persian to Arabic by Ibrahim Shiyta (Cairo: al-dhahraa lil I'lam al-Arabi 1986), pp.260-276

2. Mona Abul-Fadl, *"Nahwa Manhaageyah lil Ta'amul ma' Masader al-Tanzeer al-Islami"* [Towards a Methodology for Dealing with the Islamic Theorization Sources], in: al-Tayyb Zaiyn al-Abidiyn, ed., *al-Manhaageyah al-Islamiyyah wa al-Uloom al-Slookiyah wa al-Tarbawiyah* [Islamic Methodology Regarding Behavioral and Educational Sciences] (Hendon, VA: International Institute of Islamic Thought, 1990) , vol. 1, p. 188.

3. Mohammed Aref, *al-Manhag fi Ilm al-Igtemaa'* [Methodology of Sociology] (Cairo: Dar al-Thakafa, 1972), vol.1, p. 198.

Chapter I

ഔൠ

Comparative Methodology in Arabic Literature: The State of the Discipline

Before we begin this evaluation of the studies of Arab researchers that have dealt with comparative political theories in their efforts to analyze Arab political systems, we must address two critical issues that constitute an important prologue to good analysis.

First, a number of studies already exist that have analyzed the applicability of theories of comparative politics to the Arab political phenomena; and these studies have arrived at important conclusions that can be summarized as follows.

Halah So'udi, after studying 100 Ph.D. and MA theses submitted to the political science department of the faculty of economics and political sciences, Cairo University, concluded that:[1]

1.) Many studies, while intending to use a particular methodology, did not actually use it—or only used it selectively.
2.) Two studies only (2% of the sample) used systems analysis as the sole method of study. One used it completely and the other used it in partiality. Nine studies used this approach as a part of a multi-methodological framework. These studies did not define systems analysis or clarify how to apply it in the framework of a multi-methodological approach.

Some even used systems analysis with inconsistent methods in a kind of prefabricated admixture that was called a "complementary methodology." They used a historical approach as well as a comparative approach. They also used the social survey and the case study, as well as a structural-functionalism and a decision-making approach in one single study. At least two of these admixtures contained contradictory approaches: the comparative methodology (which needs a multiplicity of cases in order to identify generalizations) and the case study (which uses only one single case to reach generalizations.) It appeared that these partial contradictions within methods and the impossibility of joining them together in a single consistent mix were disregarded. If the intent was to use a separate method for each chapter of the study, the end result could only yield a methodological neighborhood, not a complementary methodology.

3.) Some studies that used systems analysis along with other approaches limited themselves to using the concepts of input and outputs without justifying that usage and without adopting the approach methodologically. This process empties the method of any valuable content, for those two concepts (inputs and outputs) are truisms that have no specific relation to any kind of theory. What David Easton, the originator of systems analysis, had done was provide a network of relations that turned those truisms into methodological elements. Inputs and outputs were presented in a framework of networks of concepts like the external and internal environment, transformation process, and feedback. Without these concepts, network systems analysis loses its identity and becomes general musings that represent nothing of real value in research.

In his study using class analysis, Mustafa Kamil al-Sayyd[2] surveyed the same sample as So'udi and concluded that:

1.) Very few researchers declared their intention to use a single approach.
2.) When a declaration of intention was made in the introduction, this did not necessarily imply that they used the approach. Most of these studies do not fulfill what was promised in the introduction about the approach. This reflects the minimal level of importance that methodology has in the thinking of Arab researchers, as well as the lack of knowledge about approaches in the contemporary arsenal of methodologies.
3.) Eight theses made use of class analysis. All of these assumed as true constructs that needed to be proven. These studies lacked validity in the

eyes of non-Marxist scientists.[3] What had been produced by using class analysis ideologically rather than methodologically, was ideology instead of analysis.

Al-Sayyd 'Abd al-Mutalib Ghanim[4] in his study of structural-functional analysis using the same sample as both So'udi and al-Sayyd, and concluded that:

1.) Most of the research lacked any method what so ever. However, theses were treated as if they were scientific research using the scientific method. Results were approved as if they were scientifically reliable. It is not possible, however, to build a scientific structure on an unscientific base.
2.) Very few of these studies surpassed the old approaches used in the beginning of this century. Only a minority of that small number knew what they were doing.
3.) No conceptual analysis was to be found. These studies were dominated by bibliographical antidotes and, except for a very few, were not empirical.

'Ali Layla in his study of the application of structural-functional analysis in Ph.D. and MA theses in the Departments of Sociology of the Universities of Cairo, Alexandria, and 'Ain Shams concluded that academic practice in sociology was ideologically dominated and oriented. This led to an assertion of the ideological content of functionalism; not it's epistemological aspects. This lack of demarcation between what is ideological and what is epistemological may be due to ignorance or lack of ability on the part of the researcher.[5]

In his critical analysis of the methodologies used by Arab sociologists' in their studies of societal issues in the Arab context; Salim Sari concluded that there were four main influences that transformed important issues into minor problems absent of sociological and political content in order to be in line with the paths of western and industrial societies. These are:[6]

1.) Preoccupation with western analytical concepts like societal consensus, system, function balance, and adaptation.
2.) Total preoccupation with the tools and not the philosophy of the method. We can describe Arab research from the 1950s up to the mid-1970s as functionalism-dependent within the traditional Western methods. They form such an absolute majority that any deviation from this method is a kind of aberration.

3.) A fossilized articulation of the problematic, with research issues that were mere superficial repetitions of western sociological problems. Arab researchers copied the western problematic *en bloc* as they were during the hegemony of the Chicago School in the 1920s, and applied them to the Arab context.

4.) Linkages between the research results and the interests of funding and political organizations.

f. These were five attempts to evaluate the methodology of research in political and sociological Arab academia, especially regarding the application of theories in that research. It was important to refer to them in order to understand and evaluate the results of this study.

Second, determining the essential features of the development of comparative politics in the Arab literature is an essential introduction to illuminate the background of these studies and the academic environment of the Arab researchers. The initial Arab encounter with the concepts and theories of modern political science came in the early 20th century after the first translation of a book on politics into the Arabic language in 1915.[7] This book was *Elements of Political Science* by the Canadian political scientist, Stephen Leacock, who was a professor at McGill University. It became the blueprint and idealized prototype for introductory books on politics written during the next fifty years in Egypt and elsewhere. Before that, the field of Arab politics was part of the Islamic episteme that contained different dimensions, whether in definitions, units of analysis, methods, or subjects.[8] After that, only the teaching of political science in the Islamic University of al-Azhar, continued to follow the political tradition of Islam with its emphasis on issues related to leadership (*imamah*). With the foundation of the Institute of Political Sciences in the Faculty of law at Cairo University in the early 1950s a new tradition emerged that followed the formulations of western political science as introduced through the translation of Leacock's book. That inaugural work was the first to discuss the units of analysis, concepts, frameworks, and issues that dominated politic science and still prevail in western politics today. Attempts at using these methodologies in the political literature were not widespread until the beginning of the second half of the twentieth century. What continued to take place after that was a kind of hybrid mixture of units of analysis and western concepts and Islamic terms. However, the general mood was still dominated by a traditional Islamic approach. It is in that context that we encounter the political writings of M. H. Haykal, 'Ali 'Abd al-Raziq, 'Abd al-Raziq al-Sanhuri, and others.

Since the foundation of the Institute of Political Science in Cairo University in the early 1950s, political science research continued along the lines of the western literature whether French or Anglo-Saxon. But, there was a considerable time lag. For example, during the behaviorist period in the West, traditional constitutional, legal, and historic philosophical methods dominated research in the Arab world. This was due, in the beginning, to the link between political sciences and law. It was natural for traditional approaches to dominate the studies of the pioneers until the mid-seventies. After reviewing the random sample representing all the literature that the researcher could find, we may conclude that there are two schools in Arab politics in general and political systems in particular. They are as follows:

The legal school or the trend toward constitutional and institutional analysis which dominated political sciences in the Arab world until the 1970s. The teachings of this school are still found in departments of public law in the faculties of law. It was linked to certain pioneers in Arabic political science who had studied western law in European schools (especially in France) and then transferred its principles to the field of political sciences. Their education had provided minimal contact with the political science that dominated American schools, especially behaviorism. This trend was characterized by the following[9]:

1.) Mixing principals of politics, political philosophy, political theory, and political systems in one volume, usually called "political systems."
2.) Studying formal aspects of political phenomena, namely, the state, it's structures, theories, authority, and the relation between authority and the administrative system.
3.) A total preoccupation with legal and constitutional documents and their amendments. The actual practice, however, was completely ignored.

The schools of political sciences or untraditional political analysis that went beyond legal constitutional focus and linked with new theories of American political science, especially behaviorism. This second school directed attention towards non-formal institutions such as parties, interest groups, and the other aspects and dimensions of political phenomena like electoral behavior and ideologies. It used the non-traditional approaches of behaviorism.[10] The trend was to focus on theoretical literature in comparative politics and was very much interested in defining theories and methods in the field, especially behaviorism. Its pioneers were aware of the necessity of developing Arabic political science and bringing new theories to the Arab researcher. This school of research was closely linked to professors of political sciences in the Faculty of Economics and Political Sciences in Cairo University, the mother faculty of political sciences in the Arab world. The first contribution to the literature came in 1975 and served to define political systems as a research field.[11] It presented some behaviorist theories like systems analysis, elite theory, structural-functionalism, and Marxist analysis. The second contribution in 1978 discussed all the fields of comparative politics, from definition and theory presentation to behaviorism.[12] It described the institutional legal method, group and elite method, class analysis, systems and structural-functionalism, decision-making and communicative analysis. It dealt with the different concerns of comparative politics with regard to changing formal and non-formal institutions, as well as cultural, organizational, and institutional issues. This attempt was the most comprehensive one in the field. The third contribution in 1985 was a work of research in the development of the concept of comparative politics as well as a presentation of theories such as systems analysis, structural-functionalism, communicative, and decision-making[13] These three initial works represented the first sources in Arabic literature that considered the theories of comparative politics.

After discussing political science in general and comparative politics in particular, we must define the state of comparative research in Arab political systems from a comparative perspective. We have noted that the early literature from the mid-1960s was focused on the issues of non-Arab countries such as the U.S., U.S.S.R, Britain, and France,[14] and sometimes Israel and Japan. The political systems of the main western countries were presented as if they were ideals to be followed and model to be copied. In a later development, from the 1970s some Arabic political systems were compared with major western systems.[15] During the 1980s comparisons were made between one single western state and Arab political systems. Usually the single state took up half of the research and the rest was left for the major Arab countries. These comparisons used historical or legal constitutional methods—an approach that belongs to the traditional stage in comparative politics.[16] Finally, at the end of 1980s, a new treatise was formulated that may be considered as the first to study Arab political systems using a comparative approach.[17] This research study applied cross-statal comparison using some aspects of the behaviorist methodology and going beyond the analytical frameworks that belong to the traditional stage that dominated the field of comparative politics before the second world war. This study presented theories of comparative politics and used a mixture of behaviorist and traditional approaches. It compared major Arab countries by assessing phenomena like parties, interest groups, student organizations, trade unions, syndicates, and the army, as well as formal aspects known in the field. This study was based on semi-empirical sources. In addition, it usually referred to primary sources.

With the understanding that these are the general features of comparative politics in Arab literature, we are now going to examine a number of comparative studies in depth to explore the dimensions and elements contained within them and to understand how the comparative method was used by these Arab researchers.

Standards and criteria for choosing the studies to be subjects of analysis. We will choose a group of studies to be analyzed according to the following criteria:

a. The study should be focused on comparative politics, not just a study in political science. Studies within the realms of political theories, political thought, and international relations were excluded.

b. The study must be multi-statal and discuss more than one Arab country in order to be within the Arab comparative political framework. Studies that were within the field of comparative politics but focused on one country were excluded as well.

c. The study must have been written in Arabic and by Arab authors. Translated studies of non-Arab authors were excluded, while translated studies of Arab authors were included.

We chose the publications of the Center of Arab Unity Studies, Center for Political Studies and Research in Cairo University, two magazines (*Arab Affairs* and *Arab Future*), and Masters and Ph.D. theses of the Political Sciences Department in the Faculty of Economics and Political Sciences, Cairo University, as well as MA theses of the Institute of Arab Research and Studies of the Arab League. The sample thus included books and research as well as university dissertations and covers these institutions from their inaugurations till 1994. It may be considered to be a representative sample, while not in fact providing a comprehensive cross section of most of the Arab writings in the field of political sciences. This research aims to cover the current methodological and theoretical situation surrounding the application of comparative politics in the analysis of Arab political systems.

Using these norms and criteria we identified thirty-eight studies that meet these conditions. They include:

a. Eight MA and Ph.D. theses, seven in the Faculty of Economics and Political Science and one in the Institute for Arab Research and Studies.[18]

b. Eleven books, two of them Ph.D. dissertations, and one of them published by the Center of Political Researches and Studies of Cairo University. The other eight were published by the Center of Arab Unity Studies. Each center published one of the dissertations as a book.[19]

c. Thirteen studies were published in *Arab Future* (Al-Mustaqbal al-'Arabi) and *Arab Affairs* (Sha'un 'Arabiyah); one of them was published in both magazines at the same date. It is the only study published in *Arab Affairs*, so the real number of studies is twelve.[20]

d. As for studies discussed in seminars and published within the seminars, there were ten studies, four of them published in books of the Center of Arab Unity Studies. One of them was published in the *Arab Future* periodical. The other six were published in the works of the Center of Political Research and Studies of Cairo University.[21]

Methodological rules for analysis. I will use the same rules and standards that Lawrence Mayer applied when he studied sixty-one textbooks of American universities after 1960 to determine and measure the extent of theoretical frameworks that appeared during the behaviorist period in comparative politics in order to find out to what extent researchers benefited from these theories.[22] I believe that these rules are appropriate and sufficient to analyze Arab comparative political research because they have already been tested in the same field, for the same reasons, and in regard to the same theories. These basis standards are:

a. Determine whether the research is based on real comparisons or merely on a presentation of each state, leaving the comparison for the reader. Is it based on dividing the issues into particles and presenting each state within each particle in order to measure the theoretical ability to compare holistic states, one with the other.

b. Investigate whether the studies contain discussions of comparative method and definitions of it and its provisions and strategies; not just the mere idea of comparison as an essential part of human thinking and research.[23] Applying this rule to the Arab studies, we will consider that the mere mention of "comparison" in the title is enough to include it in this study.

c. Determine whether the research in the study depends on empirical data from direct fieldwork or relies only on secondary sources. This standard has been expanded to include three categories, the first depending on empirical data; the second depending on primary sources like surveys, census, statistics, and documents; and the third depending on bibliographical secondary data.

d. Identify the theories and methods used by the researchers. Do they depend on traditional or behaviorist theories? This standard was also altered in this study. Instead of containing two categories, here it now contains four. The first is complete dependency on traditional theories and analytical frameworks, the second depending primarily on traditional theories while at the same time benefiting from the tools and ideas of behaviorism, the third depending on behaviorist theories and utilizing traditional ones, and the fourth depending completely on behaviorist theories.

e. Determine whether the study is only descriptive or is interpretational as well. As we rarely have a completely descriptive study, or vice versa, this standard was used to assess which of the two was more prevalent.

Applying the standards listed above to the aforementioned studies, yielded the following results:

a. As for the first standard, we found that twenty-one studies (55%) used complete comparison. We should look suspiciously at this ratio, however, because of the special nature of the sample. Most of the studies were published in journals or seminars. As these usually studied only one subject, it was easy to carry out complete comparison strategies within them. If we compared them with larger studies and dissertations the significance of the ratio held true as an index of the researchers' ability to do comparison completely. Among the twenty-one studies, we found six (16%) following state-to-state comparison by which they presented each state separately and let the readers make the comparisons. This strategy was usually applied within shorter studies. Comparing state-to-state within subsides was done in eleven studies (29%) and is a kind of intermediate stage between the former two. The main issue was divided into subsides and within each one the researcher presented each state separately. We conclude that there is some recognition of the importance of complete comparison due to the minimum number of studies (16%) that made simple state-to-state comparisons.

b. As for the second standard, the number of studies that could be classified as consciously comparative studies was twenty (53%). An additional eighteen studies (47%) could be classified as unconscious comparisons. Among the studies using conscience comparisons most made some mention of the concept of comparison either in the title or in the methodology. And yet, only one single[24] study discussed the comparative methodology in the introduction with descriptions of the importance of comparison, its levels, kinds, and strategies. The concept of comparison did not appear at all, either in the titles or methodologies of the unconscious comparisons. They usually did not mention any special method in the introduction. We must point out here that there is no relation between this standard and the preceding one, meaning these studies that were classified as complete comparisons were not necessarily the conscious ones. The opposite may be true.

c. As for the standard relating to the type of sources, nineteen studies (50%) used secondary sources completely. They did not use any empirical or primary sources at all. The researchers apparently were satisfied with the former studies in the same subject and they built on them uncritically. The validity of the results depends on the validity of the previous studies used, which may be nothing but entire structures of notions, results, and concepts with no inherent validity at all. Most of the phenomena in the field of comparative politics are factual and real ones. They must be studied in reality; or else these studies would be theoretical or philosophical, not comparative. Fifteen studies (39%) depended on primary, non-empirical sources like statistics and surveys and documents. Studies that were based on empirical bases did not exceed four (only 11%).[25] These are the studies that delved into reality to study it and then represent it. Their relationship with the studied phenomena was closer than those studies that depended on secondary sources or even primary, bureaucratic ones. This result shows the extent to which Arab researchers depended upon dubious sources in studying the political realities in the Arab world. They ended up with a confused mix of unorganized observations that included the researcher's own off the cuff speculations as well as the contemplation of others.

d. As for the standard related to methods and theoretical frameworks, eight studies (21%) completely followed traditional methods. They were limited to historical, constitutional and legal, and institutional analyses. Nine studies (24%) used traditional methods and benefited from some behaviorist frameworks. They used historical, legal, or institutional frameworks with some added behaviorist dimensions, quantitative tools, or structuralism. We considered those studies that used class analysis in the classical patterns as found in Marx and Engels as works midway between traditional and behaviorist approaches with more inclination towards the traditional because of neglect of recent developments in class analysis, whether on the level of Marxist thinking or non-Marxist thought. We found that twelve studies (32%) depended on behaviorist analytical frameworks with some traditional approaches. We found that some depended on the structural-functional approach, the communicative approach, or the new institutional approach, with some use of legal, historical, or class analysis in the traditional sense. The last studies were ones that depended completely on behaviorist methods—these were nine studies (23%). They made use of quantitative analysis and content analysis in the general conceptual framework of behaviorism. In addition, they also used elite theory, groups' theory, and structural-functionalism. Worth mentioning here is the fact that the nature of the phenomenon being studied often dictates the researcher's methodology, i.e.: the method that is best able to deduct the latent and exteriorized potentials in the reality, in order to reach a real understanding of its variables, causes, and effects. The nature of social phenomena in the Arab region may demand a certain methodological approach where modernity is combined with tradition and a special emphasis is placed on the historical. This led us to expand the two standards of traditional and modern as given by Mayer into the four categories mentioned above.

e. As for the last standard focusing on the issue of description and interpretation, thirteen studies (34%) went beyond simple description to provide interpretations that helped to achieve a necessary balance. We must add that while some tried to achieve a degree of balance between description and interpretation in some parts of their study, they lost this balance in other parts. For example, most researchers who engaged in some level of interpretation with regard to their own countries, failed to apply that same analysis when the research was concerned with other countries. On the other hand, twenty-five studies (66%) were only descriptive with very little analysis included. They tended to mix description with justification. Studies that used class analysis were ideal representatives of that tendency. Researchers were eager to find "evidence" to prove the existence of clear-cut class structures or at least potential ones. They were overzealous to prove that the class perspective is the best. Other studies incorporated the final results within the descriptive work of the researcher as if they were truisms that did not need to be proven. The best examples of this position were ideological studies such as the ones concerned with Arab nationalism or those that studied critical political phenomena like power transformation. They all treated these subjects as if they were given truisms.

These were the most important results of this analysis of representative comparative studies in contemporary Arab literature. We can accept the validity of these results by applying two sets of observations. The first set is concerned with the characteristics of the studies that we have chosen for examination, while the second is a general one that deals with the status of comparative research within the field.

Observations regarding the studies examined:

a. At least half of the examined studies did not achieve the level of comparison accepted in contemporary literature. They compared state-to-state, but unconsciously they followed the traditional method. They depended on secondary sources and were often merely descriptive.

b. The other half achieved better results according to the standards were using. They were completely conscious of comparison and depended on primary or empirical sources. They used behaviorist methods and they moved beyond description to interpretation. The problem is that these do not represent a coherent set of studies—they were produced in isolation from each other. Most of the studies that achieved a higher level of comparative analysis on some standards were poor in others. We can say that only one study achieved the highest levels on all standards. It was a completely conscious empirical, behaviorist, and interpretative study.[26] Two studies achieved the lowest levels: they were state-to-state, unconscious, traditional, and descriptive in comparison and they depended on secondary sources.[27] The other studies were in-between. This made it difficult to reach scientific generalizations.

c. We took the results as a general means to describe the state of the discipline. The cross-section of studies showed that there is some kind of partial response to the comparative method. This means that this episteme was known but not well understood. What exists is a kind of limited, partial knowledge and as a result, most of the studies achieved only partial results. This implies that the issues of methodology are not yet clearly understood by the researchers.

d. Empirical research got very little attention, even though it is an essential approach, especially in this field of political science.

e. There continues to be an almost complete ignorance of the goals or the essential functions of comparison. Most of the most serious studies stopped at the level of citing differences or similarities. Thus they achieved the lowest level of comparison which can not help in either interpretation or in arriving at scientific generalizations—not to mention generating theories. They did not even aspire to reach general or partial theories or reach theoretical conclusions. Most of these studies were not concerned with proving or negating theories. Only one study concluded with a theoretical remark that stated the need to reevaluate social theory based on principals regarding the notion of legitimacy as articulated by Max Weber.[28]

f. Most of the theoretical approaches used in these studies belong to traditionalism or traditional behaviorism. There is no study that made use of post-behaviorist approaches.

g. The major Arab countries dominated the scene. Egypt, Syria, Iraq, and Algeria occupied the core positions. Countries like Sudan and Yemen were never or rarely looked at. Researchers seemed to have agreed to ignore Somalia, Djibouti, and Mauritania.

General observations regarding studies of Arab political systems.
We must see the aforementioned analysis, results included, as part of a general framework because the examined studies did not represent a broad sample of the entire political research community. Rather, they are a comprehensive survey of the discipline of comparative politics. Many observations can be made to help in clarifying the results:

Arab literature in the field of comparative politics lacks a strong interest in comparing Arab systems. Comparative studies are marginalized as compared with case studies. There are particular indices that point towards this conclusion, i.e., the 'Institute of Arab Studies and Research' of the Arab League which was established in 1953. During its first fourty years, it only produced only one MA thesis comparing three Arab states with the U.S. This was a 1993 thesis presented to the Department of Legal and Jurisprudence Research and Studies, while the department of Political and National Research and Studies had never conducted any comparative studies. The same situation applies to the faculty of Economics and Political Sciences in Cairo University. Out of more than one hundred dissertations on political systems, it had only seven dissertations that used comparative methodology for analyzing Arab systems. The same applies to the most important journal of national and political studies in the Arab world, *Arab Affairs* which, in eighty issues spanning a decade and half, published just one comparative study. *Arab Future*, published seventeen years ago, had only twelve studies in one-hundred-ninety issues. The Center for Studies of Arab Unity, the only research center concerned with the Arab world in general from a politico-economic perspective, has only eight books and two seminars concerned with comparing Arab systems. On the other hand, these institutions have a surfeit of studies involving one state only or treating the Arab reality from an idealist and non-realistic perspective. They were solely concerned with what ought to be, not what is. We can attribute this lack of interest in comparative studies in Arab political systems to the following factors:

A state-centered mentality dominates academic practice, partly because of the presence of the idea of Arab Unity as an emotional and ideological element. This may be due to the real obstacles that hinder the flow of information, researcher, and communication. There is no academic framework that creates an Arab scientific community. There are only ideological frameworks that create their own sub-communities. It is natural for Arab researchers to study their own states, and difficult for them to do otherwise in depth.

The ideological dimension often overlaps the scientific research. The belief in Arabs as one nation with an eternally valid message left an unshaken belief that Arab reality was historically unified and has only now been dismantled into states. This created a vacuum in comparative studies for there is no perceived need to compare these states. It was thought to be sufficient to study one state because what applies to it would of necessity be generally applicable to others. While researchers may define a general topic for research that gives the impression they are going to include all Arab countries and begin their treatment with some general statements about the Arab world, they end by treating the issues in one country only.[29] Many researchers treat the Arab world as a single analytical unit deliberately, even though there is great diversity in social and cultural subsystems, and regardless of obvious political system variations. Halim Barakat's book *"Arab Society"* defined its analytical frame as "The whole Arab society, not just separate entities."[30] Some asserted primarily the common futures of Arab political systems and regimes.[31] This led to Arab countries being treated as if they formed a single social unit that could be studied as one entity from a political systems perspective. Or conversely, researchers believed that they could study a single state and then generalize automatically. There was no felt need for comparisons that were based on essential analysis of similarities *and* differences. Without both of these no comparison is possible.

If there is a sensitivity to researching political phenomena in the Arab world, and there is a hypersensitivity towards comparing Arab states. Comparative studies have the potential to pinpoint the facets of weakness in the countries being compared. This threatens the emotional sensitivities of state identities, bias towards one's own country, and the hypersensitivity of Arab regimes towards criticism and comparison. As well-known a researcher as Ilya Harik began his comparison between Egypt and Tunisia by actually apologizing for doing so, expressing his good intentions and his great admiration of both regimes. He declared that his aim in making a comparison was to "highlight the phenomena, their causes and results," and that he has no intention of unveiling any form of weakness in any system.[32] He then went on to praise and eulogize the achievements of all developing countries, especially Egypt and Tunisia. This shows how serious researchers consider comparison to be an act fraught with dangerous consequences— one requiring, even before starting, disclaimers and apologies. It is of no surprise then that most studies stop at description—including, in fact, very little of that—and do not continue on to interpretation.

There is no real theoretical structure in Arab comparative politics. There is very little literature in the field. The three aforementioned books had a very narrow circulation.[33] One of them is a collection of unpublished lectures, the second is very narrowly distributed, and only al-Munufi (1978) may be a little more actively circulated. Interest in theories of comparative politics is very small. As an example, the seminar organized by Arab Society for Political Sciences in collaboration with the Center for Research and Political Studies in Cairo University, entitled "Teaching of Political Sciences in the Arab world"[34] focused mainly on international relations, foreign policy, political thought, political philosophy, and political development. There was not a single example of research in the Arab political system, political systems in general, or comparative politics. It was if they were completely negligible subjects. We must note as well that most studies did not adequately use a comparative methodology. They were usually based on general ideological notions that are not proven to be true or false. They were completely unconcerned with using comparison to prove the validity of these notions. Those comparative studies that were done were conducted for justification and verification of ideological notions, rather than for scientific discovery or generalization. That may explain why only certain Arab countries were chosen as participants.

Contemplative, advice-oriented methodology dominates most of Arab political systems' studies. Researchers usually move from description to prescription in the form of general advice to all Arab countries even if they studied one country only. Hence the epistemological need for comparison is limited and minimized. Generalizations are prefabricated or researchers deduce superficial general theoretical generalizations out of small contemplative studies. It is worth mentioning that most of the titles of these studies do not really express their content. Sometimes the title is related to political systems or even comparative politics, but the content is concerned with theory or political contemplation and has no relation whatsoever with political systems or comparative politics.

These are the general external features of specialized literature in Arab political systems from a comparative perspective. What about the internal features? We will examine those in the next chapter.

Notes

1. Halah So'udi, *"Istikhdam Iqtarab Tahlil al-Nuuam fi al-Dirasaat al-Siyasiyah fi Misr"* [Applying Systems Analysis in Political Studies in Egypt], in: Wadudah Badran, ed., *Iqtirabat al-Ba'hth fi al-'ulum al-Ijtima'iyah* [Research Methodology in the Social Sciences] (Cairo: Markaz al-Bahuth wa al-Dirasat al-Siyasiyyah bi-Jami'at al-Qahirah, 1992), pp. 37-45.

2. Mustafa Kamil al-Sayid, *"Mafhum al-Tabaqah fi al-Dirasaat al-Siyasiyah fi Misr"*[Class Analysis in the Political Studies in Egypt], in: Wadudah Badran, ed., op.cit. pp. 185-204.

3. op.cit. p. 202.

4. Sayyid 'Abd al-Mutalib Ghanim, *"al-Iqtirab al-Bana'i al-Wazifi wa 'Stikhdamuhu fi al-Buhuth al-Siyasiyah: Nazarah Taqwimiyah"*[Structural-Functionalism Approach to Political Research: Critical View], in: Wadudah Badran, ed., op.cit. pp. 103-122.

5. Ali Laylah, *"al-Madkhal al-Wazifi fi Dirasat 'Ilm al-Ijtima' fi Misr,"*[Functional Approach in the Sociological Research in Egypt] in: Wadudah Badran, ed., op.cit. pp. 129-158.

6. Salim Sari, *"al-Ijtima'iyun al-'Arab wa Dirasat al-Qadaya al-Mujtama'iyah al-'Arabiyah: Mumarasah Naqdiyah"* [Arab Sociologists and their Studies of the Arab Societal Problems: Critical Appraisal], *al-Mustaqbal al-'Arabi*, issue 75, May 1985, pp. 86-92.

7. Stephen Leacock, *Elements of Political Science* (Boston and New York: Houghton Mifflin Company, 1906), Published in Arabic as: Leacock, *Mabadi' 'Ilm al-Siyasah*, translated by Salim 'Abd al-Ahad (Cairo: Mutaba't al-Hilal bi'l-Fajalah 1915). *The Canadian Encyclopdia* 1999, by McClelland and Stewart, cited Leacock as humorist, essayist, teacher, political economist born in England 1944, his first book, Element of Political Sciience, a workmanlike treatment of its subject, was his best-selling book in his lifetime.

8. About the evolution of Islamic political from early Islam till the beginning of the twentieth century see: Nasr Muhammad 'Arif, *fi Musadir al-Turath al-Siyasi al-Islami: Dirasah fi Ishkaliyat al-Ta'mim qabl al-Istiqra' wa al-Ta'sil* [Sources of Political Literature in the Intellectual Heritage of Islam: A Study of the Problem of Generalization Before Authentication] (Herndon VA: al-Ma'had al-Alamiyyah li'l-Fikr al-Islami, 1994).

9. See: 'Abd al-Hamid Mutawwali, *al-Anzimah al-Siyasiyah wa al-Mabadi' al-Distoriyah al-Aamah* [Political Systems and The General Constitutional Principles] (Cairo: Dar al-Ma'arif,1957), Muhammad Kamil Laylah, *al-Nuzum al-Siyasiyah: al-Dawlah wa al-Hukumah* [Political Systems: State and Government] (Cairo: Dar al-Fikr al-Arabi, 1967), Ahmad Sawaylim al-'Imari, *al-Nuzum al-Siyasiyah al-Hadithah lil Duwal al-Arabiyah* [Modern Political Systems for the Aeab States] (Cairo: Matabit al-Anglo al-Misriyyah, 1969), Muhsin Khalil, *al-Nuzum al-Siyasiyah wa al-Qanun al-Dissturi* [Political

systems and the Constitutional Law] (Alexandria: Monsha't al-Ma'rif, 1971), Fa'wad al-'Attar, *al-Nuzum al- Siyasiyah wa al-Qanun al-Dissturi* [Political systems and the Constitutional Law] (Cairo: Dar al-Nahdah al-Arabiyah, 1974), Ahmad Waaylim al-Imari, *Usul al-Nuzum al- Siyasiyah al-Muqaranah,* [The Foundations of comparative Political Systems] (Cairo: al-Hay'ah al-Misriyyah al-Amah lil Kitab, 1976), and Mustafa Abu Zayd Fahmi, *Mabadi' al-Nuzum al- Siyasiyah* [The Foundations of comparative Political Systems] (Alexandria: Monsha't al-Ma'rif, 1984)

10. Ahmad Kamil al-Affandi, *al-Nozum al-Hukumiyah al-Muqaranah,* [Coparative agovenment] (kuwait: Wakalat al-Matbuaat,1982)

11. 'Ali E. Hillal Dessouki, *Madkhal fi al-Nozum al-Siyasiyah al-Muqaranah,* [Introduction to Comparative Political systems] (Cairo: Faculty of Economics and Political Sciences, 1975-76)

12. Kamal al-Munufi, *Usul al-Nuzum al-Siyasiyah al-Muqaranah,* [Foundations of Comparative Political systems] (Kuwait: Sharikat al-Robai'an,1987)

13. Al-Sayid 'Abd al-Mutalib Ghanim, *al-Itijahat al-Mu'sirah fi Dirasat al-Nuzum al-Siyasiyah,*[Contemporary Directions in the Study of Political Systems] (Cairo: Dar al-Qahirah lil-Nashr wa al-Tawzi', 1985)

14. Muhammad Fath-Allah al-Khatib, *Dirasat fi al-Hukumat al-Muqaranah,* [Studies in Comparative Government] (Cairo: Dar al-Nahdah al-'Arabiyah, 1966)

15. Ni'mah al-Sa'iyd, *al-Nuzum al-Siyasiyah fi al-Sharq al-Awsat,* [Political Systems in the Middle East] (Baghdad: Sharkat al-Tab' wa al-Nashr al-Ahliyyah, 1968)

16. Hassan al-Hassan, *al-Anzimah al-Dissturiyyah fi Labnan wa Sa'ir al-Buldan al-'Arabiyah,* [Constitutional Systems in Lebanon and the whole Arab Countries] (Beirut: Dar Beirut lil-Taba'ah wa al-Nashr, 1981), and Ahmad Sirhal, *al-nuzum al-Siyasiyah wa al-Dissturiyah fi Labnan wa Kafat al-Dewal al-'Arabiyah,* [Political and Constitutional Systems in Lebanon and the whole Arab Countries] (Beirut: Dar al-Fikr al-Arabi,1990)

17. 'Ata Muhammad Salih, and Fawzi Ahmad Taym, *al-Nuzum al-Siyasiyah al-'Arabiyah al-Mu'asirah,* [Contemporary Arab Political Systems] (Benghazi: Manshurat Jami'at Qaryuns, two volumes 1988)

18. Yusaf Muhammad 'Obidan, *Nizam al-Hukm fi Duwal al-Khalij: Dirasah Muqaranah li Qatar, al-Kuwait wa al-Bahrain,* [Political System in the gulf Countries: Comparative Study for Qatar, Kuwait, and Bahrain] (Ph.D. Cairo University, 1982), Jalal Mua'wad, *Alaqat al-Qiyyada bil-Dhahiyrah al-Inma'iyah:Dirassah fi al-Mantiqah al-Arabiyah* [The relationship between Leadership and Development: A Study in the Arab Region] (Ph.D. Cairo University, 1985), Muhammad Safi-Udin Kharbush, *al-Mutagiyer al –Tanzimi fi Binaa al-Sultah fi al-Watan al-Arabi,* [The Organizational Factor in the Stucture of Authority in the Arab Political Systems] (MA Thesis. Cairo University, 1986), Neven Musa'd, *al-Aqliyat wa al-Istiqrar al-siyasi fi al-*

Watan al-Arabi, [Minorities and Political Stability in the Arab World] (Ph.D. Cairo University, 1987), Muhammad Safi-Udin Kharbush, *al-Fikr al-Qawmi wa al-Siyasah al-Arabiyah ma' al-Tatbiyq ala Misr wa Soriyah wa al-Jaza'ir*, [Arab Nationalism Political Thought and Arab Politics: The Cases of Egypt, Syria, and Algiers] (Ph.D. Cairo University,1989), Salah Salim Zarnooqah, *Anmaat Intiqal al-Sultah fi al-Bilaad al-Arabiyah1949-1985*, [Patterns of Political Succession in the Arab Countries 1949-1985] (MA Thesis, Cairo University, 1989), Hassanian Tawfiq Ibrahim, *Dhahiyrat al-Unif al-Siyasi fi al-Nuzum al-Arabiyah*, [The Phenomenon of Political Violence in the Arab Political Systems] (Ph.D. Cairo University,1990), and Hassani Muhammad, *al-Sulutat al-Istisna'iyah li-Ra'iys al-Dawlah fi al-Nizam al-Ri'assi: Dirasah Muqaranah lil Wilaiyat al-Mutahidah wa Misr wa al-Iraaq wa al-Jaza'ir*, [Exceptional Authorities of the President in the Presidential System: Comparative studies of USA, Egypt, Iraq, and Algiers] (MA Thesis, Institute of Arab Research and Studies,1985).

19. Khaldun Hassan al-Naqib, *al-Mujtama' wa al-Dawlah fi al-Khalij wa al-Jazirah al-'Arabiyah*, [Society and State in the Gulf Countries] (Beirut: Markaz Dirasat al-Wihda al-Arabiyah, 1987), Muhammad Abdul-Baqy al-Hirmasy, *al-Mujtama' wa al-Dawlah fi al-Magrib al-Arabi*,[Society and State in North Africa] (Beirut: Markaz Dirasat al-Wihda al-Arabiyah, 1987),Sa'd el-Din Ibrahim, *al-Mujtama' wa al-Dawlah fi al-Watan al-Arabi*, [Society and State in the Arab World] (Beirut: Markaz Dirasat al-Wihda al-Arabiyah, 1988), Mahmoud Abdul Fadil, *al-Tashkilat wa al-Takwinaat al-Tabaqiyah fi al-Watan al-Arabi: Dirasah Tahliliyah Liham al-Taturat wa al-Itijahat Kilal al-Fatrah 1945-1985*, [Class Formations and Structures in the Arab World: Critical Study of the Main Directions Between 1945-1985] (Beirut: Markaz Dirasat al-Wihda al-Arabiyah, 1988), Ibrahim al-Issawi, *Qiyass al-Tabai'yah Fi al-Watan al-Arabi*, [How to Measure Dependency in the Arab World] (Beirut: Markaz Dirasat al-Wihda al-Arabiyah, 1989), Khaldun Hassan al-Naqib, *al-Dawlah al-Tassalutiyah fi al-Mashriq al-Arabi al-Mu'asir: Dirasah Bina'iyyah Muqaranah*, [The Authoritarian State in the Cotemporary Eastern Arab Countries: A Comparative study] (Beirut: Markaz Dirasat al-Wihda al-Arabiyah, 1991), and Muhammad Jawaad Rida, *Sira' al-Dawlah wa al-Kabilah fi al-Khlij al-Arabi: Azamaat al-Tnmiyah wa Tanmiyat al-Azamaat*, [The Struggle Between State and Tribe in the Gulf Countries:The Crisis of Development and The Development of Crisis] (Beirut: Markaz Dirasat al-Wihda al-Arabiyah, 1992).

20. 'Abd al-Mu'ti Muhammad 'Asaf, "*Azmat al-Fa'aliyah al-Siyasiyah fi al-Bilaad al-Arabiyah: Itar nazari Muqaran*," [The Crisis of Efficiency in the Arab Countries: Comparative Study] *Al-Mustaqbal al-'Arabi*, Issue no.,36, Feb 1982, pp. 6-26 , Republished in: *Sha'un 'Arabiyah*, Issue no., 12, Feb, 1982, pp. 7-28, Sa'd el-Din Ibrahim, "*Masadir al-Shari'yah fi AnzimaT al-Hukm al-'Arabiyah*," [Sources of Legitmacy In Arab Political Systems] *Al-Mustaqbal al-'Arabi*, Issue no., 62, april 1984, pp. 93-118, Ilya Harik, "*Nushu' Nizam al-*

Dawlah fi al-Watan al-Arabi,"[The Emergence of the State System in the Arab World] *Al-Mustaqbal al-'Arabi,* Issue no., 99, May 1987, pp.77-95, Gassan Salamah, *"Quwat al-Dawlah wa Da'fihaa: Bahth fi al-Thakafa al-Siyasiyah al-Arabiyah,"* [The Strengths and Weaknesses of the State: A Study in the Arab Political Culture] *Al-Mustaqbal al-'Arabi,* Issue no., 99, May 1987, pp.96-120, al-Sadiq Sha'ban, *"al-Huquq al-Siyasiyah lil al-Insan fi al-dassateer al-Arabiyah"* [Political Rights in the Arab Constitutions] *Al-Mustaqbal al-'Arabi,* Issue no.,106, December 1987, pp. 4-24, al-Sadiq Bel'id, *"Door al-Mu'assassat al-Deniyah fi Da'm al-Anzimah al-Siyasiyah fi al-Bilaad al-Arabiyah"* [The Role of Religious Institutions in Supporting the Political Systems in the Arab Countries] *Al-Mustaqbal al-'Arabi,* Issue no.,108, feb 1988, pp. 70-84, Hamid Anssari, *"Hudood al-Sultah al-Khassah bil-Nukhabal-Hakimah: al-Tama'tu' bi-Sultah Datiyyah fi Manzur Muqaran"* [The Limitations of Ruling Elite's Authority: Comparative Study] *Al-Mustaqbal al-'Arabi,* Issue no.,113, July 1988, pp. 44-58, Ilya Harik, *"al-Dawlah al-Ra'wiyah wa Mustqbal al-Tanmiyah al-Arabiyah,"*[The Patriarch State and the Future of the Arab Development] *Al-Mustaqbal al-'Arabi,* Issue no.,121, March 1989, pp.4-28, Intwan Nasri Massarah, *"Tanziym al-Ilaqah biyna al-Din wa al-Siyasah fi al-Anzimah al-Arabiyah al-Mu'asirah: Bahth fi Nazariyah Amah Istinadan ila Halati Lybnan wa Misr"*[Systemization of the Relationship between Religion and Politics in the Contemporary Arab Political Systems: The Cases of Lebanon, and Egypt] *Al-Mustaqbal al-'Arabi,* Issue no.,131, Jan. 1990,pp. 70-88, Salah Salim Zarnooqah, *Anmat Intiqal al-Sultah fi al-Nuzum al-Wirathiyah al-Arabiyah1950-1985,* [Patterns of Political Succession in the Arab Monarchical Systems1950-1985] *Al-Mustaqbal al-'Arabi,* Issue no., 140, October 1990, pp.72-95, Ahmad Thabit, *"al-Ta'adudiyah al-Siyasiyah fi al-Watan al-Arabi,"* [Political Pluralism in the Arab World] *Al-Mustaqbal al-'Arabi,* Issue no.,155, Jan. 1992, pp. 4-20, and Abdul-Latiyf al-Hirmasi, *"al-Harakat al-Islamiyah fi al-Mgrib al-Arabi"* [Islamic Movements in North Africa] *Al-Mustaqbal al-'Arabi,* Issue no.,156, Feb. 1992, pp. 15-31.

21. Sa'd el-Din Ibrahim, Masadir *al-Shari'yah fi Anzimat al-Hukm al-'Arabiyah,"* [Sources of Legitmacy In Arab Political Systems] in: *Nadwat Azmat al-demucratiyah fi al-Watan al-Arabi,* [Seminar on The Crisis of Democracy in the Arab World] (Beirut: Markaz Dirasat al-Wihda al-Arabiyah, 1984), Abdul-Qadir Zagal, *"al-Mujtam' al-Madani wa al-Sira' min Ajl al-Himana al-Idulogiyah fi al-Magrib al-Arabi,"* [Civil Society and the Struggle for Ideological Hegemony in North Africa] in: *Nadwat al-Mujtam' al-Madani fi al-Watan al-Arabi wa durahu fi Tahqiq al-Demcratiyah,* [Seminar on Civil Society in the Arab World] (Beirut: Markaz Dirasat al-Wihda al-Arabiyah, 1992), Haidar Ibrahim Ali, *"al-Mujtam' al-Madani fi Misr wa al-Sudan"* [Civil Society in Egypt and Sudan], in: *Nadwat al-Mujtam' al-Madani,* op.cit., Baqir al-Najar, *"al-Mujtam' al-Madani fial-Khalij wa al-Jazeerah al-Arabiyah,"*[Civil Society in the Gulf Countries], in: *Nadwat al-Mujtam' al-*

Madani, op.cit., Kamal al-Munufi, *"al-Tanshi'ah al-Siyasiyah wa Manzumat al-Qiam fi al-Watan al-Arabi: Dirasat Halah lil-Tanshi'ah al-Madrasiyah fi Misr wa al-Kuwait"*[Political Education and The Value System in the Arab World: A Case Study of Elementary School in Egypt and Kuwait], in: Mustafa Kamil al-Sayid, ed., *al-Tahawlat al-Siyasiyah al-Hadithah fi al-Watan al-Arabi*, [Contemporary Political Changes in the Arab World] (Cairo: Markaz al Buhuth wa al-Dirasat al-Siyasiyah bi-Jama'at al-Qahirah, 1989), Hoda Mitkiyys, *"al-Shar'iah wa al-Mu'arada al-Diniyah: Dirasat Halaht Misr wa al-Magrib,"* [Legitimacy and Religious Opposition: The Cases of Egypt and Morocco], in: al-Sayid, ed., *al-Tahawlat al-Siyasiyah al-Hadithah fi al-Watan al-Arabi*, op.cit., Neven Musa'd, *Idulujiyat al-Aqliyat wa Azmat al-Dawlah al-Arabiyah al-Mu'asirah: Dirasat halat Suriyah wa al-Sudan"* [The Ideologies of Minorities and the Crisis of the Modern Arab State], in: al-Sayid, ed., *al-Tahawlat al-Siyasiyah al-Hadithah fi al-Watan al-Arabi*, op.cit., Muhammad Safi-Udin Kharbush, *"Ru'iat al-Qiyadah al-Libiyah lil-Demucratiyah: Dirasah Muqaranah ma' Ba'd al-Tajarib al-Arabiyah"* [The Libyan Leadership Perspective on Democracy: A Comparative Study With other Arab Countries], in: Neven Musa'd, ed., *al-Tahawlat al-Demucratiyah fi al-Watan al-Arabi,*[The Transition to Democratic in the Arab World] (Cairo: Markaz al Buhuth wa al-Dirasat al-Siyasiyah bi-Jama'at al-Qahirah, 1993), Ikram badr el-Din, *"al-Ta'dudiyah ala al-Mostwa al-Nazari: Dirasat Halati lebnan wa al-Sudan"* [The Theory of Pluralism: A study of The Cases of Lebanon and Sudan], in: Musa'd, ed., *al-Tahawlat al-Demucratiyah fi al-Watan al-Arabi,*op. cit., and Ibrahim Awad, *"al-Azmah al-Iqtisadiyah wa al-Ihtijaj wa al-Tatawur al-Demucraty: Dirasah Muqaranah lil-Jaza'ir wa al-Ardun,"* [The Economic Crisis and The Transition to democracy: A Comparative Study of Algiers and Jordan], in: Musa'd, ed., *al-Tahawlat al-Demucratiyah fi al-Watan al-Arabi,*op. cit..

22. Lawrence C. Mayer *"Practicing What We Preach: Comparative Politics in the 1980s," Comparative Political Studies*, vol.16, no.2 July 1983, pp.173-194.

23. Else Oyen, *"The Imperfections of Comparisons"* in Else Oyen, ed., *Comparative Methodology: Theory and Practice in International Social Research* (London: Sage Publication, 1990) pp.3-4.

24. Mua'wad, op.cit.

25. al-Munufi, *Usul al-Nuzum al-Siyasiyah al-Muqaranah*, op. cit., H.T.Ibrahim, op. cit., al-Issawi, op. cit., and al-Hirmasi, op. cit.

26. H.T.Ibrahim, op.cit.

27. Zaghal, op. cit. And Hassani Muhammad, op. cit.

28. Harik, *Nushu' Nizam al-Dawlah fi al-Watan al-Arabi*, op cit. 95.

29. Manal Yunus al-Samrai', *al-Mar'ah wa al-Tatwur al-Siyasi fi al-Watan alArabi*, [Women and Political Progress in the Arab World] (MA Thesis, Institute of Arab Research and Studies, 1988).

30. Halim Barakat, *al-Mujtam' al-'Arabi al-Mu'asir*, [contemporary Arab Society] (Beirut: Markaz Dirasat al-Wihda al-Arabiyah, 1986), p.29

31. Yahya al-Jamal, *"Anzimat al-Hukm fi al-watan al'Arabi,"* [Political Systems of the Arab World], in: *Nadwat Azmat al-demucratiyah fi al-Watan al-Arabi*, op.cit. pp. 355-370.

32. Harik, *al-Dawlah al-Ra'wiyah wa Mustqbal al-Tanmiyah al-Arabiyah*, op.cit. p. 5.

33. Dessouki, op. cit, al-Munufi, *Usul al-Nuzum al-Siyasiyah al-Muqaranah*, op. cit., and Ghanim, op. cit.

34. Abdul Mun'im Sa'iyd, ed., *Tadris al-'Ulum al-siyasiyah fi al-Watan al-'Arabi*, [Teaching Political Sciences in Arab world] (Cairo: Markaz al Buhuth wa al-Dirasat al-Siyasiyah bi-Jama'at al-Qahirah, 1990).

Chapter II

ഇൻ

Attempts to Adapt and Develop Theoretical Frameworks to Study Arab Political Systems

This study has discussed the general state of comparative politics within the Arab academia in the previous chapter and concluded that there are a very limited number of these studies. They are quite rare within the huge corpus of Arab political literature and depend mainly on analytical frameworks, methods, and theories that belonged to the pre-behaviorist period, viz. a viz. the western methodological heirloom of pre-World War II. The essential epistemological issue here relates to the following questions: Were theories of comparative politics sufficiently well known in the Arab academia? In other words, was there any significant familiarity with western literature from the field of comparative politics or was there a gap in the field? Was this gap a result of researchers' attitudes towards these theories and their epistemological foundations? Or was it a dimension of the crisis of underdevelopment in Arab societies which showed very little interest in scientific research and insisted on transforming science into ideology along with an almost complete rejection of epistemological matters of significance for ideological content? It is not impossible that the motivations of researchers dealing with these theories comes more from belief, than from utility and usage. Beliefs served as a window for sacralizing the theory and for fanaticism that could lead to a complete rejection of reality or to reducing it to fit one theory or another. Utilization and usage leads to understanding and the ability to adapt theories to fit with reality, instead of the other way round.

This problem requires a serious effort to analyze certain cases that reflect the major models used by Arab researchers for dealing with theories of comparative politics. Their choices in using certain theories to study the Arab reality can include a degree of intentionality. For this reason, research approaches that limited themselves to formal adaptations of any of these theories were neglected. An example of this would be using an Arabic concept like *surat* instead of elite[1] which makes it possible to Arabize elite theory by finding a traditional Arabic concept to use in place of the modern meaning of the elite.

We shall focus here on two essential attempts that represent two models of using or adopting comparative theoretical frameworks to study Arab political systems.

Adapting class analysis to study Arab political systems. Class analysis is considered to be one of the most controversial theories of comparative politics, because of its relation to philosophy, ideology, and political movements. It also varies in content, dimension, and outlook.[2] Class analysis can be employed as an analytical approach in social sciences, as a philosophy to explain history, and as an ideology that demands that reality either conform to or be changed to fit into its commitment to historical determinism. In its ideological application distorted reality is taken out of history, and moved into the depths of dogmatism, so as to fit into one of its theoretical stages. While many developments have accrued in the methods and the criteria used for the identification of classes, i.e. ownership, income, vocations, and living standards, according to orthodox Marxism there are only two opposing classes. In contemporary liberal sociology you can find nine classes. Because of its continuous development in the literature, whether of Marxist or Weberian-Parsonian perspectives, a number of questions arise: What is the position of these developments in the methodology of comparative politics in the Arabic literature? How do they interact with class analysis? From what angle, methodological or ideological, do they approach class analysis?

The following will present two major works that show the ideas of authors making use of class analysis, without any attempts at rearrangement of their approaches:

a. The first work[3] represents an effort to present all of the contributions that were present in the literature related to studies in class structure in the Arab world. The ideas of the author about the identity of class analysis and how to adapt it to study Arab society were propagated in several parts. We shall present this study as the author did it, then we shall give general and detailed criticism.

Abd al-Fadil begins by pointing to the diversity of the concept of class in western thinking whether Marxist or Weberian. He then proceeds to examine class classification and social stratification in Arab historical literature. He refers to Ibn Khaldun who asserted the importance of social affairs in the development of human *'umran* (civilization). He cites al-Naqib in his analysis of the identification of four levels of social identification as described by Ibn Khaldun: identification by clan or tribe, identification by religion, identification by profession, and identification by place or region.

He then concluded with a citation from the covenant of Imam 'Ali ibn Abi Talib with his governor of Egypt al-Ashtar al-Nakha'i, that divided society to three classes: administrators, including judges, ministers, and civil servants, the military, and people who pay *kharaj* (a sort of tax from the land's crops).

'Abd al-Fadil defines *kharaj* as the economic surplus that the state depends on for funding such needs as renovating and enlarging the military. 'Abd al-Fadil cited parts of the text he referred to and neglected other parts and rearranged the text. In short he mutilated the text. The complete text as cited in 'Abd al-Fadil's research reads as follows: "People are classes. They need each other. They are soldiers of Allah, officials, judges, civil servants, tax collectors, traders and professionals, and the needy. God has provided for each. God provides for all. The ruler is obliged to provide each of them with something to straighten him.[5]"

We can easily notice that the text gives a broader number of classifications than that of 'Abd al-Fadil, and on different bases. Because these classes depend on mutual cooperation and alternating roles they need each other. There is more than one criterion for classification, such as profession, status, economic situation, and income. There are actually seven classes according to the text: military, high officials, judges, civil servants, tax collectors, traders and professionals, and the needy.

Abd al-Fadil then returned to Ibn Khaldun as interpreted by Muhammad 'Abid al-Gabri's analysis. Al-Gabri thinks that, except for the Bedouins, Ibn Khaldun divides society into two classes:[6] the elite which was comprised of rulers, wealthy men, officials, scientists, and poets (this is a non-productive class that lives on the money of the ruler); and the common which was comprised of peasants, artisans, and traders.

Here also we can see clearly how simplistic and reductionary this re-classification is. In his writings, Al Naqib pointed out that the levels of identification in Ibn Khaldun influence the concept of stratification. He clearly stated that Ibn Khaldun does not divide society into two classes because of his view of social taxonomy where the horizontal classifications intermingles with the vertical ones due to intersecting standards of identification like religion, profession, or region. Al-Gabri and 'Abd al-Fadil have adopted a procedure that is known as the collection of opposites and unification of contradictories in order to reach a binary taxonomy that aligns with an ideological hypothesis. Here, however, we encounter addition questions: Why were the Bedouins excluded although they were not a minority in that time? Why and how were rulers, wealthy men, officials, scientists, and poets included in one class? These considerations help to clarify the doubtful and imprecise nature of this classification. 'Abd al-Fadil concluded, however, by emphasizing a central notion in Ibn Khaldun—the dialectic relation of money and status or authority and power. This idea is contrary to the Marxist analysis that sees a single unidirectional relationship only. The belief that power is a result of money or property and not vice versa[7]is noteworthy. However, 'Abd al-Fadil's next analysis did not consider this and did not utilize it in adapting and developing comparative class analysis.

The study moves on to present modern attempts to classify Arab social classes. It begins by discussing the French scholar, Andre Raymond, and his encyclopedic work "Artisans et commercants au Caire au XVIIIe siecle" Raymond studied *awqaf* (endowments) and jurisprudential records. He concludes his work by presenting a quaternary classification of classes: the class of quotidian workers, the class of petite artisans, the class of middle artisans, and the class of trade bourgeoisie.

Raymond concluded by saying that the Cairene society had witnessed a movement of integration between categories of artisans, traders, rich men, and the military ruling class of Turks in the 17th and 18th centuries. They even called the later Misr-ly meaning the Egyptianized one[8] (*misr* is Arabic for Egypt). A. Fadil also presented the work of Habib al-Ginhani[9] in which he divided Moroccan society of the 9th and 10th centuries into five classifications: traders, military, scientists, slaves, and poor people.

This review of literature discussing class analysis in Arab society clearly shows that the criteria of class classification varied. Most depend on standards of living, status, income, profession, religion, and jobs. While the Marxist criterion of capital ownership was very limited. After reviewing all of these historical facts 'Abd al-Fadil concludes that the elements of class structure and class relations in Arab societies are intermingled with elements of tribal structure. Because of this, there is always confusion between a horizontal class structure and a vertical tribal one.[10] He then questioned the validity of dominant theoretical frameworks in Western sociology, whether bourgeoisie or Marxist (but mostly the Marxist notions), to understand and explain Arab society. Before responding, he reviews some of the works that tried to address this problem. He begins with 'Abd al-Qadir Zaghal,[11] who criticized academic practices in the Arab world as being locked into Weberian and Marxist traditions. Zaghal said that both belonged to the same tradition of the great transformations in Western Europe in the 19th century. He pointed out the fact that Arab sociologists, by the end of the twentieth century, had limited themselves to importing those frames of reference and tools developed exclusively to satisfy the needs of western culture in the 19th century—while Ibn Khaldun and the founding fathers of modern sociology had creatively formulated their own tools appropriate to their own time. 'Abd al-Fadil reviews as well the conclusion of el Maliki: "Debate about social classes in the Arab countries is usually made in terms that were more significant for Europe in the 19th century than for third world countries in the 20th century. Countless Arab efforts to justify the existence of feudalism and bourgeoisie using Marxist measures have meant defining ourselves according to Europe not to ourselves"[12]

These answers highlight considerable concern over the application of theories that had originated and developed in specific and different historical contexts. There are difficulties facing research that attempts to apply orthodox Marxist analysis in the contemporary reality of the Arab world. However, 'Abd al-Fadil concluded by saying, "Although this criticism is valid, there is always a general validity for historical materialism in studying class structure in the Arab world. The problem lies in the negative application and the absence of a real and creative application of that method." He thinks that the real challenge lies in "enriching and adapting historical materialism to fit within a new set of historical, social. and economic facts."[13]

He goes further to criticize the proposed mosaic model for studying the Arab world. He even criticizes Marx himself for using the concept of the Asian mode of production as a tool to analyze non-western communities. And he goes on to emphasize the possibility, even the necessity, of using historical materialism to study the Arab world[14] because "the method of historical materialism remains the most important key to understand the developments that happened to social formations within Arab countries."[15]

As we can see, the conclusion of 'Abd al-Fadil is not consistent with his introduction, whether in regard to the nature of historical or contemporary class classification in the Arab world, or to criticisms of analytical frameworks using class analysis in its orthodox Marxist sense. The material that he presented initially asserts that Arab reality is completely different epistemologically from the European historical reality.

Throughout its history class classification in the Arab world was based on standards different from Marxism's. Although contemporary literature of class analysis is different and diverse with much epistemologically Marxist analysis implied, traditional scholars usually made use of non-materialistic categories. 'Abd al-Fadil regresses epistemologically and methodologically with an empirical overflow that completely ignores the developments within the episteme. He returns to the thesis of the young Marx who based his historical materialism on negating the independence of political and social phenomena, considering both of them as dependent variables. For Marx these phenomena are mere reflections of the materialist structure of reality which is composed of the tools of production that create relations of production.[16] The result is a complete rejection of the autonomy of the state and political phenomena, canceling out consideration of the state as well as the civil society producing it[17]

In conclusion we can easily see that ideology has conquered epistemology in this case. The researcher flouts reality even in his important attempt to survey history. He also ignores both the Arab literature which he surveyed, that tried to explore the validity of applying class analysis in its orthodox Marxist style, and the developments of class analysis in western literature as well. He asserted the ideological validity of class analysis by going back to the philosophy that produced it in an attempt to bypass the binary Marxist taxonomy of classes, forgetting that using historical materialism in a coherent way can only lead to the end results of the early Marxism. Although this work declared that its aim was to adapt class analysis to the Arab situation, it ended by justifying and marketing an orthodox Marxist analysis which has already been bypassed by contemporary Marxist discourse.

b. The second work differs from the first one in that it does not comprise a survey for literature, criticism, or review. It consists of the research presented in a seminar that proposed the Marxist perspective as the best model among western methods to study political phenomena in the Arab world.[18] M. K. al-Sayid began by discussing the arguments for rejecting western perspectives, whether Weberian-Parsonsian, or Marxist. He differentiated ethnocentrism and what he called the general heritage of humanity that ought to be a benefit to the field of social sciences. He considered the rejection of these perspectives as being an ideological position that totally contradicts the scientific method and he enumerated the errors of this rejection as follows:

1.) Lack of differentiation between the scientific method and the content of certain scientific disciplines.
2.) Equating the Weberian-Parsonsian, and Marxist schools when the first is the formal representative of the western trend in the studies of third world that justifies the continuation of hegemony, and the second is a tool in the liberation of the working class that has contributed to the liberation of the third world.
3.) Continuous confusion between three distinct aspects of Marxism: its political application, its perspective on the study of history and reality based on certain propositions, and its theoretical efforts to interpret social and historical development.
4.) Confusion between Marxist analysis of the capitalist mode of production in western Europe and its view of general developmental paths and the right Marxist analysis of third world reality. As the colonies did not occupy Marx's attention, he objected to attempts to enlarge and generalize his view of the development of Western Europe to provide a universal view of human history. His analysis of the Asian mode of production assumed that the past of the colonies differed from that of Europe. Hence their paths of development must have differed as well.[19]

These introductory remarks spoke in general about western approaches. From the second remark onwards, however, western was equated with Marxist. The points that were mentioned contradicted each other and confused things, much as they had been criticizing others for doing. For example, the second remark negates the others because it justifies the Marxist approach as being a liberating theory, not the formal colonial western one. Here we encounter confusion between ideology, method, and politics. There is also confusion about the three aspects of Marxism. The fourth remark is a kind of objection to the study, as we shall see.

After this, M. K. al-Sayid presented evidence to prove that there is no valid absolute universal theory, and concluded by saying that total rejection and total acceptance are non-scientific positions. He considered any attempt to reject or accept any theory without studying it thoroughly to be non-scientific. He then presented ideas that he considered as originating from a 'researcher with a scientific spirit'. These were the ideas represented by the Marxist contributions to understanding the Arab reality. He asserted that because Marxism does not contain scientific research tools, it does not force the researcher to leave behind one's own tools of social science.

He also said that Marxism uses a perspective, called dialectic materialism, that points to certain aspects of social phenomena. He summarized the features of dialectic materialism as follows:

1.) Unity of nature, including human activity—all that is present in the universe of matter, plant, animal, or human constitutes a single unity.
2.) One critical human activity is the effort to produce the necessities for existence. In the last analysis, it is this process that determines the kind of social, political, and ideological structures necessary for that activity.
3.) Evolution is an essential feature of matter and society. Evolution happens through mutations that represent qualitative transformations that are preceded by an accumulation of quantitative ones.
4.) The principal of unity and struggle of opposites asserts that each form of matter contains its opposite and has a certain internal tension.[20]

He concluded by saying that dialectic materialism presents the best method for studying the Arab political reality.[21] We can clearly see that this presentation as well suffers from internal contradictions. It gave an introduction that is never logically realized in the conclusion of the study. He began by rejecting any attempt to accept or reject a theory without applying it and testing it on the grounds of being unscientific. On the other hand he accepted dialectic materialism as the best method suitable for studying Arab reality without applying it and testing it.

Hence we can judge him by his own criteria as non-scientific. If he had said its application was valid only in Europe, this would have been consistent with what he asserted in his introduction about the absence of a universally valid theory.

His view of the researcher with true scientific spirit is another questionable and ambiguous matter. Ideas in science must have empirical validity, and yet for him, if they originate from a truly scientific researcher, they become philosophy. Another question here is who is going to decide that the researcher has this true scientific spirit and based on what criteria? This study represents a more severe regression than that of 'Abd al-Fadil which had adopted historical materialism. This study adopts dialectical materialism, which is a philosophy that explains the origin of universe and matter. While historical materialism is the application of dialectical materialism in history using the same laws of matter, dialectical materialism is not possible without historical materialism and vice versa. We cannot have universal dialectic materialism unless we can interpret social life materially and unless we discover that society is just a more complex form of matter and its movement, under control of the same objective material laws.[22] Hence we can see that dialectic materialism and historical materialism represent a philosophical system for interpreting the movement of universe, nature, and society. Regarding either one of them as a method to study and interpret Arab society entails confusion between method and philosophy or between scientific and philosophical theory. Dialectic materialism can be considered to contain its own metaphysics because it is based on hypothetical notions that cannot be proven logically or empirically. Presenting it as a method to study Arab reality is ideology. It is neither methodology nor science.

In a more developed argument, M. K. al-Sayid presented the class perspective directly as a theory to study and interpret political phenomena in the Arab reality.[23] In the beginning of this presentation he talkes of "the importance and necessity of destroying the dominant confusion between class perspective and Marxist analysis. Those who followed this perspective in western literature at least are not all Marxists. Some even are anti-Marxist. Although Marxist contributions to the understanding of class structure in western and third world societies are well known, accepting the class perspective does not necessarily imply accepting Marxist analyses. It may only imply acceptance that the basic unit of analysis in society is the social class."[24]

Later on, M. K. al-Sayid presented the class perspective as a theory to better interpret and compare political phenomena than other perspectives like groups or elites. He said, "stratification is a feature of most societies. The concept of class is well suited to comparative studies unlike concepts like group or elite, for the identity of many ethno-social groups varies from society to another. Elites differs according to states. But there is always a proletariat and capitalists (or the large property owners in many societies). If it is difficult to compare the behavior of an Iraqi Shiite, for example, with other Shiia, we can more easily compare the behavior of working classes across the societies of the third world, even across the world."[25]

This attempt tries to promote the classical Marxist class perspective which is based on property ownership and divides society into two classes, those who own and those who do not own and sell their labor force. Hence all this talk about separating class analysis and Marxism and the contributions of non-Marxist, even anti-Marxist philosophers, did not influence the conclusion. It was simply used as a justification and promotional tool in order to sell the class perspective—which was presented as a commodity that was competing with theories of groups and elite. The argument suggests that we ought to use one perspective only, even when dealing with multi-faceted and complex reality. Each of the alternative theories, however, has its own field, issue, and levels of analysis. Although the author judges group theory through a narrow application chosen by himself, theories of groups or elites can be used to compare groups in different parts of the world simply because they emphasize groups regardless of their nature or identity. They can compare, for example, ethnic groups, peer groups, or violent religious groups regardless of ethnic identity or religious affiliation. Thus, trying to present group theory through the example of Shiite groupings is reductionistic and leads to a narrowing of the theory.

These were two efforts that attempted to present class analysis as the best theory to be utilized in studying, interpreting and comparing politico-social phenomena in the Arab world. It is clear that the authors had adopted the classical view of the class analysis as presented by Marx. They were ideologically dominated and they ignored important epistemological aspects of society. If they had considered the latter aspects, they might have arrived at a formula for adopting class analysis so as to make it more valid in studying Arab reality.

The civilizational perspective: A new approach to the study of Arab political systems. This attempt to develop a theoretical framework that utilizes a civilizational approach to the to study Arab polities[26] has three main dimensions as follows:

a. It was presented in the context of a university curriculum for final year students in a department of Political Sciences, and is therefore at the core to the developing field of comparative analysis of Arab political systems. It was applied and tested through four years of study, from 1981 to 1984.

b. It is an attempt that focuses on presenting a methodological introduction to the direct study of specific Arab polities without reference to a general framework that encompasses all political phenomena or Arab society in general.

c. It is an authentic adaptation attempt as well as a new approach that is worth consideration and analysis in dealing with social sciences in general in the Arab world. It is not based on ideological acceptance of analytical frameworks and epistemes of the west. At the same time, it also does not reject ideologically these frameworks and epistemes. Instead, it deals with them epistemologically, as originating from paradigmatic knowledge.

In this way, theories of comparative politics become an epistemological source that can be understood, analyzed, and interpreted while remaining cognizant of their paradigms and neutralizing their biases in order to reapply them in other systems.[27]

This effort combines the specificity of phenomena in Arab political systems, their historical-cultural dimensions and the communication and complete usage of theories that dominated the episteme of comparative politics in western literature without falling into the trap of biases, either "for" or "against."

This approach contributes to the negation of polar ideologies like tradition and modernity, original and foreign, past heritage and contemporaneity. It holds that the problem is essentially epistemological and depends on understanding and cognition. The goal is to develop and construct theoretical frameworks that add these dualities without exclusion in order to makes it possible to see the studied phenomena as the basis for analysis, and utilize the frameworks as tools.[28]

We find that this work contains three groups of issues, the first relating to justifications that necessitate this approach, the second relating to the bases and epistemological foundations for this approach, and the third dealing with this approach itself and how to benefit from theories of comparative politics. We will present these issues in the following context:

Two sets of reasons and justifications are proposed in this work. The first set comes out of Arab reality and the second out of global reality.

1.) Subjective justifications coming out of Arab reality, i.e., the concrete situation of Arab polities. Mona Abul-Fadl sees many aspects of Arab society as passing through a crisis. This crisis takes the form of simultanious identity, legitimacy, effectiveness, and integrity crises. It is evidenced by cases of extreme polarization, dissociation, and contradiction. Current Arab society is effectively without civilizational efficacy although it has tremendous potentialities. It has lost direction and found itself in what she termed a "vacuum equation"—a state of vacuum in content related to identity and direction. Because of this the society is pulled by momentum and gravity into other containment circles. The society may alleign itself with other civilizational entities which have different cultural and political systems like the west or with previous historical paradigms like previous civilizations such as Pharonism , Barbarism, and pabelism. This transitional situation with its multiple elements and factors necessitates an orignal methodology. Adding to the difficulty, is the situation of contemporary Arab thinking, which is passing through the same crisis as the political and social reality, and has filled its methodological and ideological void with epistemological frameworks coming out of other civilizational contexts. Under these circumstances theoretical frameworks take the form of ideologies which are unable to develop and grow in the Arab reality. Another justification comes from academia, which depends mainly on the acceptance of European historical paradigms without practicing essential deconstruction and criticism.

2.) Objective reasons out of the global reality relate to methodology itself and how it deals with Arab society. A viable methodology must recognize the multiple and diverse issues involved in overcoming real problems, and thereby give legitimacy to attempts towards *ijtihad* (creative renewal). It must accept that methodological frameworks that correlate with the Arab reality will differ from western ones. Just as there is diversity within the western scientific structure, there is nothing that prevents researchers studying non-western societies from using analytical frameworks that depend, in their basic notions, on their own cultural structures and still benefit from western methodologies.[29]

The second set of issues asserts the process of using the civilizational perspective as a point of entry while focusing on its basic epistemic introductions as follows.[30]

The epistemological bases of this methodological approach which represents its truisms and postulates as follows:

a.) Emphasizing revelation as a source of knowledge and clarifying how it has influenced the origin and path of Arab identity throughout history. Revelation represents the primary source of the first Arab polity. The structure of Arab society reflects the central position given to revelation as an original constitutive organizational source. Thus, this methodology must be based on the truism that there is a vital role for religion in the Arab socio-political life.[31]

b.) Expanding on the above position, the civilizational perspective weighs the cultural dimensions as well as the epistemological aspects of political phenomena. This is based on a view that insists on asserting the interaction and correlation of all variables and aspects of social phenomena without describing any of them as the only independent variable. According to the civilizational perspective, a political phenomenon is not a mere reflection of the economic situation, as in Marxism. The economy is not seen as a completely independent phenomenon without relation to social and cultural structures of society. It is an interactive phenomenon within a social reality with a context based on interdependence.[32]

c.) Thus the development of society is ruled by the logic of a civilizational dynamic which is neither a dialectical nor a historical materialism. The source of motion is the will not the matter. According to this concept, human beings are the originators of social motion because they are free and responsible. Progress is linked primarily to the human efficacy and moral realization of the society, not to the material dimensions of existence.[33]

d.) Societal motion in the western epistemic system runs in a single progressive direction with some tensions but with no change in its linear nature. This belief underlies the five Marxist stages as well as the ideas of progression and development in non-Marxist western thinking. On the other hand the motive logic reflected by the historical experience of Islam is based on the idea of circular, helical motion. Society goes into commutative circles of ascending and flourishing then descending and declining, and so on. If western researchers see that as stagnation, the civilizational perspective asserts the doubleness of this historical movement It is similar to the motion of the solar system, which combines circularity and ascendance while moving from point to point.[34]

This work developed a set of concepts that were integrated with concepts adapted from theories of comparative politics. Among these concepts we find " socio-civilizational entity," which was considered to be the basic unit of analysis. It is defined as "a multi-dimensional concept that reflects the spatio-temporal, material, and value dimensions within a unique formula. It is an abstract concept that can represent any human group which forms a single organic entity that has a common consciousness due to common geographical, historical, and civilizational factors."[35] In addition, concepts like civilization, environment, motive, legitimate state, and civilizational efficacy are all included.

This attempt focuses on redefining politics. It goes on to compare between the basic concepts in the western epistemic system, which are power, freedom, authority, equality, and the state; with those of the Islamic historical experience, like *khilafa (*vicegerency*), imama* (leadership*), maslaha (*human interest*),* and *adle* (justice).[36] The legitimacy issue in the Islamic perspective rests on two principals, power and right, wherein right comprises all of the teleologically higher values such as justice which control political practice, while power reflects those contents related to tools or means such as authority, dominance, and submission. Right is linked to the idea of what should be (in Arabic *al-wujub*) and power is linked to efficacy (*tamkin* in Arabic). Through the rules that govern *wujub* and *tamkin* as they apply to right and power we are able to deal with legitimacy from a different perspective.[37]

The third set relates to the adaptation and usage of some theories of comparative politics. Mona Abul-Fadl considered her framework a kind of combination that is comprised of both civilizational and developmental perspectives. Thus she tried to utilize all theories of development in order to build the civilizational perspective using the following denominators:[38]

1.) Re-thinking the major aspects of development theories in order to apply those concepts used in systems analysis, structural-functionalism, and communicative analysis that serve to enrich the analysis of Arab political systems, while taking into consideration the basics and truisms of each.

2.) Using the civilizational perspective to identify special concepts linked to state in the Arab and Islamic experience.

3.) By integrating analytical tools chosen out of modern schools, with issues coming out of areas of cultural traditions of the region, the civilizational perspective is able to deal with issues of comparative politics.

With this approach, Mona Abul-Fadl was able to benefit from the systems theory of David Easton using the concepts of inputs, outputs, and environment. Linking all of them to the systems memory of Karl Deutsch, she transformed the concept of memory to the political group as a represention of the environment of the political system, with its element of subjectivity. The concept of environment was enlarged to cope with ramifications of time, space, and civilization.[39]

Abul-Fadl also used the concept of systems abilities, found in the structural-functionalism of Almond, to analyze the relation between social entity and political system. She considered their harmony to be essential as a source of political coherence through integration of the parts and unification of movement towards subjective aims. This coherence between entity and system is the tool for coherence in the function of the system and the key to achieving a balance between their elements and motion. It is the source for defining the aims of the society.[40]

She also utilized some aspects of dependency theory through considering the idea that the continuation of political as well as economic dependency is linked to the ability of the dominant partner to influence the centers of self consciousness of the political group and destroy its will. The system will follow partially or totally all the aims of the hegemonies of the dominant partner and all the outputs would be in its favor. In the long run, a gradual separation between the political system and the civilizational social entity occurs, and dependency factors isolate them and destroy political efficacy. The society experiences escalating clashes between systems and the entity.[41]

These are the important features of this third work. We should not yet see it as a comprehensive theory. It is still at the stage of assumptions with only a few examples and models. It needs to be applied to several cases in a comparative perspective to verify its validity. Many of its original concepts need to be defined more clearly so they may be utilized in actual studies of Arab political systems.

Notes

1. Iliya Hariq, "*al-Suratiyah wa al-Tahuwil al-Siyasi fi al-Mujtam` al-Arabi,*" [The Elite and Political Change in the Contemporary Arab Society] *Al-Mustaqbal al-`Arabi,* Issue no. 80, October 1985, pp.4-21
2. Nasr Arif, *The Re-enchantment of Political Science : Theories of Comparative Politics, An Epistemological Approach,* (Binghamton:State University of New York Press, Forthcoming)
3. Abdul Fadil, op.cit.
4. Khaldun al-Naqib, "*Binaa` al-Mujtam` al-Arabi: Ba`d al-Furud al-Bahthiyah*" [Constructing The Arab Society: Some Assumptions] *Al-Mustaqbal al-`Arabi,* Issue no. 73, September 1985, p. 26
5. Abdul Fadil, op.cit.p. 22
6. Ibid., p.23
7. Ibid., p.23
8. Ibid. pp. 25-26.
9. Ibid. p. 26
10. Ibid. pp. 28-30.
11. Ibid. p. 37.
12. Ibid. p. 38
13. Ibid. p. 39.
14. Ibid. p. 50.
15. Ibid. pp. 43-57.
16. F. Kaylali, and M. Kufalzun, *al-Madiyah al-Tarikhiyah,* [Historical Materialism], translated from Russian to Arabic by Ahmad Dawud (Damascus: dar al-Jamahir, 1970), pp. 9-16
17. Burhan Ghaliyun, *al-Mihnah al-Arabiyah: al-Dawlah Did al-Umah,* [The Arab Dilemma: The State Against the Nation] (Beirut: Markaz Dirasat al-Wihda al-Arabiyah, 1993), pp. 9-10.
18. Mustafa Kamil al-Sayid, "*Manahij al-Bahth al-Garbiyah wa Dirasat al-Waqi` al-Arabi ma` Isharah Khasah lil-Marxiyah,*" [Western Methodologies and the Study of the Arab Reality with Special Reference to Marxism], *Nadwat al-Ulum al-Siyasiyah fi al-Watan al-Arabi* [Paper Presented at seminar on Political Sciences in the Arab World] (Cyprus: Arab Association of Political Sciences, February 4-8, 1985.
19. Ibid. pp. 2-5.
20. Ibid. pp. 8-11.

21. Ibid. pp. 12-17.
22. Kaylali, and Kufalzun, op. cit. p. 12
23. Mustafa Kamil al-Sayid, "*al-Manzur al-Tabaqi wa Dirasat al-Dahiyrah al-Siyasiyah*," [The Class Approach and the Study of Political Phenomenon] in: Ali Abdul-Qadir, ed., *Itijahat Hadithah fi Ilm al-Siyasah*, [New Directions in Political Science] (Cairo: Markaz al Buhuth wa al-Dirasat al-Siyasiyah bi-Jama'at al-Qahirah, 1987).
24. Ibid. p. 43.
25. Ibid. p. 45.
26. Mona Abul-Fadl, *Madkhal Minhaji fi Dirasat al-Nuzum Al-Siyasiyah al-Arabiyah*, [Methodological Approach For the of the Arab Political Systems] (Cairo: Faculty of Economics and Political Sciences, 1982) vol.,1-2
27. Arif, *The Re-enchantment of Political Science*, op. cit.
28. Abul-Fadl, op.cit. vol.2, pp. 4-5
29. Ibid. vol.1, p. 8
30. Ibid.vol.2
31. Ibid.vol.1, pp. 66-95.
32. Ibid. vol.1, pp. 21-28.
33. Ibid. vol.1
34. Ibid.vol.1, pp. 104-107.
35. Ibid.vol.1, p. 28.
36. Ibid.vol.1, p. 10
37. Ibid.vol.1, pp.58-64
38. Ibid.vol.1, pp.22-23
39. Ibid.vol.1, pp. 19-20.
40. Ibid.vol.1, pp. 31-32
41. Ibid.vol.1.

Chapter III

ഔ

Reconstructing a Theoretical Approach for the Study of Arab Political Systems: Epistemological Foundations

We can clearly see the gap between Arab literature in comparative politics and the state of the art since the behaviorist revolution. This gap may be due to an acute crisis resulting from the unsuitability of the analytical tools available. It may have come about because of neglecting the importance of theorization in preparation for the study of political phenomena, whether comparatively or not. This is often the result of not having a solid scientific tradition that produces studies controlled by methodological assumptions appropriate for interpreting reality and developing theory or methods in accordance with it. Differences and variations in phenomena demand a transformation and adaptation of methods and theories. Cantori said, "If we appear to have a 'kit bag' of paradigmatic tools, how are we to know which ones to employ? The choice involves the appropriate 'fit' between analyst, paradigm, and the subject of analysis."[1]

This triple relationship should be coherent. As the reality and the researcher are not subjects of choice, the element that should be brought into harmony with reality is the paradigm and its analytical tools. It is necessary to build a theoretical structure to integrate these elements. Coherence leads to efficacy in analysis, precision in interpretation, and validity in understanding. This theoretical structure needs first of all to have epistemological foundations that have been questioned and verified. If these foundations can achieve agreement and consensus from among the academic community, they will become the basis for an applicable theoretical framework.

I will pause here to present a set of introductory ideas that serve to draw attention to research in certain problematic areas that have been encountered in the effort to build a theoretical structure applicable to Arab political systems.

1. When building paradigms, theories or research approaches are very important. We cannot understand or analyze phenomena without them. And we cannot do scientific research unless we follow the principals underlying the application of these scientific instruments. These sets of methodological tools are used to define and form knowledge in order to facilitate the process of communication between members of the scientific community.[2] In order to use them effectively we should consider the following:[3]

- There is no single theory or paradigm that can be universally applied for interacting, in a balanced manner, with all of the important aspects of changing and contradictory social reality.

- Theories are not to be judged as being true or false. They should be evaluated with regard to the extent to which they help the researcher to see reality. They may be less helpful or more helpful. Hence they are either valid or not valid.

- The existence of incomplete methodological guides, or ones that are incoherent, is better than their absence. We must recognize their incompleteness, however, if further study of reality is to help develop more complete methodologies.

2. Theories of comparative politics are not essentially contradictory or competitive. They may be integrative and complementary if the researcher understands them and defines their content, assumptions, and truisms. One can utilize them either piece by piece or in an integrative way to define precisely the identity of the phenomenon that is best suited to the methodologies of one theory or another. Those that cannot be dealt with effectively, call for a search for other methodologies. One should know which are most suitable for each stage of research or for each of the aspects of social phenomena. Much effort has already been expended to classify theories of comparative politics, considering each of them as arising out of

a certain dimension of social phenomena. One classification arranged these theories into four major groups:[4] systems theories, cultural theories, development theories, and class theories.

Another work classified theories of comparative politics into three oppositional pairs:[5]

State-centered theories versus society-centered theories. State centered approaches are as old as comparative politics itself. They focus on the state, institutions, constitutions, and relations between authorities with very little interest in informal institutions such as interest groups and parties. This approach is descriptive, usually legal or historical. It has focused primarily on the major western countries. This approach became outdated at the end of the second word war. After that, attention shifted to the social content of politics. The focus of this research was directed towards studying popular participation, media, election behavior, public opinion, and the rules and bases of political life. The works of G. Almond, Verba, and most of the behaviorist contributions come under this category. In the 1980s attention shifted again towards the state. A major trend in comparative politics began to see state not as an institution but as an active mediator for effecting change in society. This new trend studied the effects of the state in society instead of describing formal state institutions.[6]

Political systems theories versus political change theories. The first of these focuses on stability and continuity and how to reach stable, continuous relations between government and society. The second focuses on change, such as developmental issues and political transformation. This model of political systems theories is David Easton's enlargement of the traditional institutional approach that opened the door for concepts coming from mechanics and latter on linked those with systems analysis. Easton looked primarily at the political system, not the government. He shifted the attention of politics away from governmental institutions and towards studying the relation between government and society. On the other hand, class analysis looks at the dynamics of social and political change.[7]

Theories of political process versus theories of public policies. Most theories of comparative politics address political process not policy. For example, systems analysis looks at the process that is used to transform demands into decisions rather than identifying the content of the demands that were transformed into policies by the political system. The 1970s and 1980s witnessed A growth in the interest of political scientists in policy per se. Analysis was focused on outputs, that is to say, public policies. This was a return to Harold Lassewell's definition of politics. "Who gets what, when, and how." This approach is more suitable for comparison, because it leads to the interchangeable benefits between compared states. Successful policies in each of them can be applied in others.[8]

Through these classifications of theories of comparative politics we can clearly see that each one is a partial theory that tries to put forth one single aspect of a political phenomenon as being most comprehensive. Perceiving the core of the theory and its focus helps to define the issues most relevant to it and, conversely, the theory that will be most effective in analyzing particular issues. Analyzing and deconstructing the theory is crucial to defining its epistemological dimensions, initial assumptions, the social context in which it appeared, and issues that gave rise to the theory and were transformed by it. Determining its truisms will lead to a better understanding of the theory and a better ability to define issues that are best suited to its methodology.

3. There is a dialectical relationship between theories of comparative politics and political reality. Transformations of these theories do not come as a result of a direct, teleological relationship between theories of comparative politics and the dominant concepts or paradigms of science. A change in the latter does not necessitates changes in the former. Besides the effects of changes in the structure of science and paradigm on the theory, there are other aspects of reality to be studied. For example, in the 1950s and 1960s, most theories of comparative politics were dominated by the behaviorist paradigm. Most applications of these theories were done in the frame of development, its crisis, and strategies. In the post-behaviorist stage with increased interest in outputs of political processes especially the studies of public policies, the issues studied were environmental issues, family, gender, women, social relations, social groups, ethnic groups, racism, and others. Theories of comparative politics became more interested in such aspects of society as corporatism, the state-society relation, and political economy. Any review of the studies published recently in comparative politics shows a clear regression toward traditional issues like political education, political culture, participation, parties, interest group, policy making, and the emergence of contemporary issues like pollution, gender, women, and family.

Perceiving this fact necessitates that we begin by identifing the phenomena and research problems of the Arab political reality that are worthy of consideration. After this, research should focus on finding effective and suitable methodological, analytical, and theoretical frameworks to explain and interpret them. If there are no appropriate theories, we must adapt and create methodological frameworks that can deal effectively with the phenomena under consideration. By building these frameworks from the real phenomena and testing them in reality we will be following along the path of the founding theoretical frameworks.

4. According to H. Wiarda, the field of comparative politics since the 1970s has become more dissociated. There is no single dominant paradigm today as compared with developmentalism in the 1960s. There is not even one theoretical structure that is accepted by most researchers. With increasing criticism and rejection of the developmental model, comparative politics lost its former unity and a state of theoretical plurality dominated. This has produced islands of theories, with multiple entry points and multiple paradigms.[9]

This state of dissociation in the field of comparative politics is not outside the western epistemic system in the stage of postmodernism. Since the mid-1980s, six key words repeatedly appeared in social sciences literature. They are: "post," as in post-modernism, post-positivism, post-behaviorism, post-communism and post-structuralism; "end," as in end of history, end of liberalism, and end of communism; "transition from" as in transition from totalitarianism and transition from authoritarianism; "transition to," as in transition to market economy and transition to democracy; "deconstruction," and "reconstruction." These words show that the current stage is at a crossroads with the period of great transition that happened in western epistemic structure in the 19th century with Marx, Weber, and others.

So, we are facing a general transitional state with no fixed formulation at any level, whether theoretical or paradigmatic. Even the skeleton of the evolving international system exemplifies this situation. The position of having neither theoretical nor paradigmatic agreement means that there is a possibility of developing, adapting, and building theories in the field of comparative politics without fear of being outside of a universal scientific consensus. This can create opportunities for the acceptance of new contributions to the literature in the field, as happened with Latin American thinkers who have developed more than one new theory. Their initiatives are now fashionable within most research communities in both the third world and the developed countries (which had monopolized the production of theories for such a long time.)

5. Scientific thinking—which involves defining the problem, putting out assumptions, gathering data, analysis of data, and interpretation, which lead to results that increase predictability—is enhanced by differentiating between various theories as stepping stones that lead the human mind to

reach knowledge through scientific research. This process is summarized as the scientific method. The concept of method implies a framework that sees phenomena from certain angles. It is a multidimensional concept, as multiple as these entry points and angles are. There is a quantitative method, qualitative method, empirical method, cultural method, communicative method, decision-making method, and systems method. These are the partial presentations of the abstract concept of method, which is single and universal. These models are not singular, however. They are not universal and they are not general or valid for every issue.

Each applies the general rules of the scientific method in a certain framework through certain truisms and assumption, and even prejudices. This leads to the proliferation of what are called methods of scientific research. We must differentiate between those two aspects of science. Attaching the adjectives "universal" or "scientific" to any or all of the methods of the western epistemic system is neither precise nor true.

For example, when Sayyid Yasin discussed with Brono Etienne, a French professor, an MA thesis of a French researcher who used the concept of civil society in the study of conflict between Shari'ah and law in Egypt and Syria, the professor responded by objecting to the use of the concept, although he had used it himself. Etienne said that civil society is a Hegelian concept and is linked to European history, hence it is not suitable in Egypt. Yasin rejected that position on the grounds of unity in method—that there is no difference between "developed" and "backward" societies from the perspective of cultural analysis. If, for example, the problem of backward societies is modernity and the problem of developed societies is post-modernity, there are many similarities between them. This makes the difference quantitative not qualitative.[10] The notion of unity of method has no epistemological, methodological, nor realistic grounds. It is based on an ideological position that assumes the unity and linearity of human history— that all societies must march forward on a progressive linear pathway. Some of them lie behind the others and others sit comfortably in front. Based on this assumption, the current Arab world is living in the period of early modernity (with Hegel, Marx, and the others) and the west is living in post-modernism. Hegelian concepts would therefore be best for the Arab reality. This concept has been disputed, however, both realistically and historically. Even the central notion of post-modernity refuses the standardization of western experience or Eurocentrism.

6. The problematic of the relationship between theory and reality. It is accepted that theory must emerge out of reality and must be tested on the

ground in order to be adapted to the needs of reality and its variables. But this relationship is not always unidirectional. It is not always reality that changes and develops theory because there are other aspects of the theoretical process to be taken into consideration.

Theory, after complete building and testing, changes into a tool with which to see parts of reality. The results of a study do not reflect reality as it is, with all the elements, relations, interactions, and relative weights embedded in it. A study and its results are merely reflections of those elements, entities, and relations that responded to the theoretical framework and passed through its concepts, postulates, truisms, and variables. If there had been a change, adaptation, or mutation in the theoretical framework, the results would have been different.[11] Theory usually rearranges elements and variables and gives them different relative weights that may not be present in reality. Theory supposes that some of these variables are independent and others are dependent. This is a theoretical postulate, which may not be true for this or that phenomenon.

Usually reality responds to some extent to any theory because phenomena are complex and all elements and variables play a certain role with their differences being in their relative weights. Theory stresses certain variables and redefines their roles, which gives the impression that theory conforms to reality. The truth is theory formed reality to fit itself. In so doing, it destroyed and mutilated much of that reality.

Theory may practice a certain kind of methodological blackmail on researchers. That is to say, it may push them towards ignoring elements that do not correspond with its analytical framework. The researcher may be well aware of the importance of these elements, nevertheless he may ignore them and puts them out of the research because they are not compatible with one's theory, or because the tools and concepts of that theory cannot cope them. Applying quantitative analysis on certain phenomena may lead to this contradiction. In a study concerned with the measurements of the total power between the Arabs and Israel, the religious and ideological aspects were ignored and removed from elements of power because they cannot be fitted within a quantitative analysis. This was done even though these elements play an important role, especially in determining total Israeli power—Israel originated directly out of these ignored elements.[12]

For this reason, reality must be decisive in determining the framework of analysis that can cope with it. The nature of the phenomenon studied will define the amount of quantity and quality required by the analysis being used. When studying the role of ideology in totalitarian systems, for example, one speech by Hitler or Stalin may be enough and represents more than hundreds of papers and thousands of articles. The quantity of information alone can creates a false belief in its scientific truth.[13]

Continuous use of certain analytical and theoretical frameworks may give them a scientific seal although they are not compatible with reality. The influence of scientific research, which is distorted by an ideological message that effects the conscious tools of individuals or groups, can disturb the relative weights granted to elements and variables in society and lead to segregating specific social phenomena. Both the individual and the group can be pushed in directions that may create phenomena, which are reflected in their analytical frameworks and considered to be real when they are not. In this case, theory functions like a self-fulfilling prophecy.

7. Science does not know the final word. Absoluteness is not a function of science. It has no absolutes. Each element is subject to criticism, and it is possible to change and go beyond every element. Science is a continuous search. Science seeks to discover parts of the truth or most of the truth. It cannot become disenchanted with the truth and, at the same time, it does not have claim to all the truth. This awareness must inform all aspects and dimensions of research so as to allow it to continue as the basis for developing science and the finding of vital paradigms. Turning theories into absolute ideologies with ultimate validity is outside of science and its project.

8. Establishing a standard for evaluation is a problematic that faces the comparative method at all levels. Comparison between two units is based on considering one of them as a standard for the other, or measuring both against a third outside standard. There must be an ideal system within each theory to represent a standard for evaluation. This standard may be a political system or ideal type coming out of the conclusion of sets of systems, ideas, historical experiences, or cultural systems. In the presence of the cultural, civilizational, and social diversity in the world, it is very difficult to identify a standard universal system. Before utilizing a theory outside of its cultural context, we must first define the standards that have been applied in order to neutralize them.

9. There is the possibility of developing pathways that can lead to founding non-standardized theoretical frameworks from certain standards that were thought to be ideal models to be used to measure all cases of comparison. The most important of these pathways is to utilize some dimensions of the concept of syllogism,[14] which is one of the tools of science of the *usul al-fiqh* (the Islamic legal theory) to apply rules to reality. The dimension that can be used for our purposes is the concept of teleology,

which can be understood as the underlying wisdom (*hikmah*) or reason behind any social phenomenon. The teleology of political parties, for example, is to maximize the citizen's power in dealing with the state, and provide a counter balance to the governing body. The teleological concept of comparable purposes, when used in comparative methodology, is one of the best entrance points to overcome the problem of standardization. It can inculcate comparative politics literature with a new approach that will negate the impact of ethnocentricity.

This will provide the possibility of reaching non-standardized comparisons valid for all political systems without bias toward a specific model. Here comparison will not be made because of the presence of institutions, structures, or functions. Rather it is going to be made according to the wisdom or the teleology behind the presenting phenomenon, such as parliaments or parties. For example, if the wisdom behind the idea of parliaments is to assure the accountability of the governing body, or to prevent dictatorship, this may be an entry point for comparison. The researcher can search for the presence of this same purpose even though it may be realized in different modes according to the demands of diverse societies. Here the reason is the same but the forms are different.

Borhan Ghalion[15] has applied a similar methodology in his study of the problem of the state. He abstracted the state as a real fact to three levels that represent the core of the state concept or its teleology. These levels are:

- The central apparatus used by an authority, which may be a national republic or monarchy, or mercenary groups or drug smugglers, and so on.
- The rules that limit and regulate the execution of power, and manage its transfer among those who possess legitimacy to control the apparatus. These rules are not the product of will or law; they are the fruit of historical experience with social power.
- The underlying moral vision that gives the polarity between ruler and ruled it's meaning, and draws its horizon in the social consciousness. This is the realization of a higher humane principal, whether this ideal is relegated by the divine with the aim of building a theocracy or by the drive to achieve the maximum level of individual freedom as an ultimate moral aim. These higher values foster the presence of political consensus and give the state another point of reference that strengthens its internal equilibrium.

These three levels may not exist in all countries. Some may have only the first level, in which case the state becomes an delicate external layer that can easily be broken. Hindered by the absence of any one of these levels, it is difficult for the state to achieve any real accumulation of national organizations, traditions, or values.[16]

We can consider these three levels of abstraction of the identity of the state to be its teleology. Reference to this can allow for comparisons between different states, without taking any one of them as a standard and without being biased toward any particular historical experience. This abstract method of comparison contrasts with contemporary political theory, which views the state in accordance with the experience of the nation-states in the west, where identity is usually constructed according to one nationality, using one language, and based on one ethnic origin. We cannot compare between this type of state and the imperial states found in many parts of the world that were brought under colonial occupation.[17]

10. There is a set of dimensions and aspects that are unique to the Arab society. They represent structural elements in the political entities of that society. We can summarize them as follows:

The epistemology of the traditional Arab political entity was different from the racist, national movements that sought the unification of a people of one race within a single nation-state in the style of Bismarck in Germany. Nor was it developed as a result of a class revolution or a military coup. The Arab state developed within an epistemological framework that was related to the emergence of Islam and the shifting of the fragmented tribal loyalties of the Arabs into a liberating mission that included others who were beyond national or racist absolutes. As containment was achieved within a general framework that was based on unity reflected through diversity, the state evolved without deforming or abolishing cultural specificities. Arab unity was traditionally based on ties that were represented by and presented in the Arabic language; together with the cultural, educational, and scientific frameworks relevant to Islam. The elements of this unity held its component parts together despite the presence of differing political frameworks, borders, passports, customs houses, and artificial sovereignties that have been realized over time. Moreover, this historical model was accompanied by an economic unity where markets were related and exchange of goods carried out among all Arab countries. As cultural factors and economic dimensions came into play they demonstrated the capacity of social activities to form a strong, integrated bases for political unity. At the same time, these inter-relationships represented and supported the existence and continuity of the Arab political entity.[18]

The Arab political entity did not witness ruling regimes based on specific racist dogmas or fixed geographic boundaries. The Arab state emerged as a system that focused the peoples' loyalty and attracted them to its norms because it gave them civil rights and added to the economic, social, and religious freedoms that they enjoyed. Elements of flexibility were present in the system that allowed for constructive interaction with the traditional patterns of the people of these areas where they were developed, present and vitalized.[19]

According to the Islamic paradigm, religion cannot be considered as a variable in the same way that political, economic, social and cultural variables are considered. This refers to the fact that religion in other paradigms was an additional element that was added to the existence of a society at one of the early stages of its evolution. The Arab experience exhibits a case where religion was the causal factor behind the establishment of the Arab political entity. The entire history of Arab civilizational, social, and political entities was linked to a religious vocation. The result of this vocation was the establishment of a political entity that led to a cultural and intellectual unification of the different elements of the pre-existing Arab society. Religion is not an element or a variable the way other elements or variables are. It cannot be separated in a manner similar to that of economic variables and the like. Religion is the backbone upon which all vertical pillars are created. These pillars are represented by political, economic, social and cultural variables. Religion gives these variables their content, in one way or another.

The level of religious influence over variables other than religion varies according to time and social stratification. It remains, however, as a fundamental and unchanging reality influencing all other variables. Religion in the Arab society is not measurable as an experience unrelated to the goings on of the world. It is unlike the religious experience wherein religion is a mere element among the various experiences absorbed by the society after the completion of its civilization. An example of this later process was the introduction of Christianity into the Roman civilization.

The permanent presence of history in the collective Arab awareness makes history an essential element that should be considered when dealing with phenomenon existing in the Arab reality. Accordingly, it is impossible to draw a sharp line of demarcation between what is traditional and what is modern, what is historical and what is contemporary or even between what is Islamic and what refers to pre-Islamic cultural frameworks.

History in the Islamic paradigm has many manifestations. It is the reservoir of human experience as it is reflected in popular heritage. History is the source for inducing the general laws that govern social phenomenon.

It shapes today's world and gives the basis for many possibilities in the future. Accordingly, placing any political notion or institution within its historical context and investigating its components, major themes and principal ideas is essential.

The great rupture between state ideology and the culture of society started during the era of Mohammed Ali in Egypt and was characterized by the serious attempt to build a modern state with characteristics of the western model for education, industrialization, and legislation. A deep divide developed in Egyptian society turning it into two separate entities, one being that of a narrow intellectual elite who were educated in and lived according to western knowledge, values, and language. The wider portion of Egyptian scholars, who remained steadfast to the inherited culture that had safeguarded the mental and psychological balance of the people, represented another level of stratification. The intellectual leaders of the masses were those who had a deeply ingrained Arab culture linked to the epistemological resources of the nation. The graduates of al Azhar, el Zaytouna, and al Qairawan universities represented that counter-elite. Thus, a crystallization of tradition developed along side of the process of modernization and Westernization taking place in most of the institutions, organizations, knowledge, disciplines, and the cultural patterns of society. In this sense, two coexisting but conflicting paradigms were being developed. Each was trying its best to abort the activities of the other. The overly lengthy competition between the two parties became intellectually exhausting with the result that neither of them could achieve full victory over the other or full domination over society on its own. The continuation of this situation led to the dramatic failure of the Arab project, which had tried to make use of a number of opposing and contradictory factors that led to its final destruction. Such a contradictory status produced to a permanent collision between state and society, not only on the political level but on the intellectual and cultural ones as well. The Arab State could not activate or vitalize the potentialities of society, and society could not cope with or coordinate with the state. The apparatus of the state was expanded at the expense of society. Eventually the state engulfed most of the societal activities that used to preserve the integrity and well being of society. Society was no more independent than the individual. It became linked tightly to a static apparatus, as the state became the sole farmer, manufacturer, merchant, teacher, doctor, and holder of the drops of water, and circulator of the air, and even mediator between the man and his wife. In this sense, the Arab state turned into a fully authoritarian apparatus that not only lead to total bankruptcy of the society, but also came to regard dominating and controlling the various aspects of society as the primary objective for its existence.

Contradictions in the relations between state and society were the main cause for successive failures in the attempts of Arab political systems to achieve further development. These failures were due to the same factors that led to the rupture between the ideology of the state and the culture of society that were mentioned earlier.

The elements of failure in all Arab projects were quite similar to those that occurred in the case of Mohammed Ali's project in Egypt—which collapsed in 1839 after the intervention of the western powers. The same elements were present at the collapse of the Ismail Pasha project in 1882 which lead to the colonization of Egypt. The next liberal development project met the same fate in 1948, and the Nasserist attempt collapsed totally in 1967. Although we cannot predict what will happen in future, this experience indicates that considerable attention should be given to the nature of the relationship between the culture of society and the ideology of the ruling regime when dealing with Arab political systems. This relationship should be considered as one of the most critical determinants of future success of failure.

The concept of state is a fragile one within the Arab mentality. Historically the Arab state has always been an artificial political entity that does not reflect concrete geographical realities or specific socio-political entities. The Arab state was not defined as separated and independent of its surrounding territories the way the European state was. The State in the Arab experience consisted of temporary reigns of elite dynasties.

Last but not least, out of these introductions—and due to them— we can begin to build, adapt, and develop theoretical frameworks that contribute to the study of Arab political systems in an effective way. This means that contemporary comparative studies being conducted with a limited focus on Arab states should consider all of those states. They should be spatio-temporal comparisons that, once tested and proved valid for analysis and interpretation, seek to reach conclusions and generalizations that may turn into theories. In this way, we can build a theoretical structure originating out of the Arab political reality, that communicates with the cultural and ideological heritage of Arab society and also benefits from the dominant literature in the field of comparative politics—in order to achieve our objective of harmony between paradigm, research, and subject.

Notes

1. Louis Cantori, *"Post-Behavioral Political Science and the Comparative Politics,"* in: Louis Cantori, and Andrew Ziegler Jr., eds., *Comparative Politics in the Post-Behavioral Era* (Boulder, CO: Lynne Rienner Publishers,1988), p.419

2. Karl Popper, *The Logic of Scientific Discovery* (New York: Science Editions, 1961) pp.49-56

3. Stephen White, Johon Gardner, Georg Schopflin, and Tony Saich, *Communist and Postcommunist Political Systems: An Introduction*, (New York: St. Martin's Press, 1990) p.20

4. Ronald Chilcote, *Theories of Comparative Politics* (Boulder, CO: Westview Press,1981), p.7

5. Rod Hague, and Martin Harrop, *Comparative Government and Politics: An Introduction* (London: Macmillan Education, 1987), pp.20-27

6. Ibid., pp.20-22

7. Ibid., pp.22-26

8. Ibid., pp.26-27

9. Haward Wiarda, *"Toward the Future: Old and New Directions in Comparative Politics,"* in: Haward Wiarda, ed., *New Directions in Comparative Politics* (Boulder,CO: Westview Press, 1991), pp.242-245

10. Al-Sayid Yassiyn, *"Wahdat al-Manhaj fi Dirasat al-Mujtamaat al-Mu'sirah"*[One Method for the Study of Contemporary Societies], in: Neven Musa'd, ed., *al-Aalamiyah wa al-Khussusiyah fi Dirasat al Mantiqah al-Arabiyah*, [Globalism and Particularism in the Study of the Arab World] (Cairo: Markaz al Buhuth wa al-Dirasat al-Siyasiyah bi-Jama'at al-Qahirah, 1991), p. 30.

11. Manfred Niessen and Jules Peschar, eds., *International Comparative Research: Problems and Methodology, Methodology and Organization in Eastern Europe* (Oxford: Pergamon Press,1982), pp.45-46

12. Jamal 'Ali Zuhran, *Manahij Qiyas Quwat al-Dawlah ma' al-Tatbiyq ala Tawazun al-Quwah bina al-Arab wa Isra'iyl*, [Methods of Measuring the State's Power and It's Application on the Power's Balance between Arabs and Israel] (Ph.D. Cairo university,1988).

13. Carl J. Friedrich, *"Some General Theoretical Reflections on the Problems of Political Data"* in Richard L. Merrit, and Stein Rokkan, eds., *Comparing Nations: The Use of Quantitative Data in Cross-National Research* (London: Yale University Press,1986), p.58

14. Muhammad Suliyman Dawud, *Nazariyat al-Qiyas al-Usuli Manhaj Tajriybi Islami: Drasah Muqaranah*, [Analogy in Islamic Legal Theory as an Experimental Method] (Alexandria: Dar al-Dawah, 1984), pp.21-31

15. Ghaliyun, op.cit., pp. 29-33.

16. Ibid. p. 33.
17. G. Lowell Field, *Comparative Political Development: The Precedent of the West*, (New York: Cornell University Press, 1967) pp.4-5
18. Abul Fadl, *Madkhal Minhaji fi Dirasat al-Nuzum Al-Siyasiyah al-Arabiyah*, op. cit., Vol. 1, pp.5-7
19. Ahmad Tirbin, *al-Tajzi'ah al-Arabiyah: Kaiyfa Hadathat Tariykhiyan?* [Arab fragmentation: How did it develop historically?] (Beirut: Markaz Dirasat al-Wihda al-Arabiyah, 1987), pp.21-23

Chapter IV

ഇരുഠ

Elite Approach as a Model for Theory Adaptation to Study Arab Political Systems: Potential and Problematic

The political systems found in the Arab world are, to a great extent, dependent on the characteristics and composition of the elite. Since there are no well-defined rules for the political process in Arab societies, governance and the state-society relations have been dominated by the role of the elite in the systems of governance. Elite theory therefore is the most appropriate approach to analyzing and understanding contemporary Arab political systems. If the class or group approach were to be used, it would become apparent that there are no well-defined class structures or well-defined groups in the Arab countries as compared to western political systems. In this chapter I will examine elite theory to illustrate its methodological potentialities for application in the Arabic context as a model for the adaptation of a theory of comparative politics in non-western society. The main theme here is the validity of this theory for understanding and explaining the political phenomena of the Arab world. In this chapter four major points will be addressed: the epistemological postulates of elite theory; the potentialities of applying elite theory in the study of Arab political systems; the problematics highlighted by using elite theory in studying Arab political systems, suggested plan for developing elite theory for the study of Arab political systems.

The epistemological postulates of elite theory. Elite theory, one of the theories of the transitional phase between traditionalism and behaviorism, has maintained its methodological vitality and its academic credibility even beyond the behaviorist phase due in part to its well-established approach to understanding and analyzing political systems.[1] In the following I will condense the most important epistemological determinants and components of this theory.

a. Dependency of the political phenomenon. According to class analysis—which has been regarded as the epistemological foundation of elite theory—the political phenomenon should be understood as a dependent variable to the modes and relations of production. The same is true for elite theory, since the understanding and analysis of a political phenomenon can only be achieved by understanding and analyzing the existing social structure, while bearing in mind the assumption that a small group of individuals controls the state and society. Thus, this elite group forms and shapes the political phenomenon, determining its dimensions. As a result, scientific analysis should focus on this group, considering it to be the proper entrance to the understanding and analysis of the political process or the political system as a whole. It is in this sense that elite theory differs from other theories in comparative politics such as the structural-functionalism, system theory, decision making, and others. These alternative theories are based on the assumption of the full independence of the political phenomenon, which can therefore be analyzed and understood through an exclusive focus on its internal structure, its self-interactions, and the nature of relations among its components parts.

b. The horizontal hierarchical classification of society. Elite theorists, as well as class analysts, assume societies to be hierarchical structures classified horizontally into classes or strata according to economic or non-economic measures. In all cases, the vertical classification of the society into races, ethnic groups, regions, and religions is not admitted into consideration. Both elite and class theorists have concluded that these vertical classifications neither influence the structure of the society nor determine or explain its phenomena.

The horizontal aspects of social structures are considered by those theorists when studying a society because they correspond with the idea that societies should be classified into strata or classes within which competition and struggle are the main logic of interaction. Accordingly, in each society, some rule and others are ruled. This horizontal societal struggle is believed to determine the content and direction of the political process.

Therefore, to understand the political system, it is important to understand the nature and structure of the horizontal social classification, together with the pattern of relations between the higher and lower classes and the main characteristics of the ruling class.[2]

c. Concentration of power in the hands of a minority. Regarding "power," elitism and pluralism are quite contradictory in their epistemologies. Elite theory assumes that power is concentrated in the hands of a single small group of people in society. On the contrary, pluralism is based on a set of assumption that understand power as being shared by diverse groups. While the pluralistic distribution of power might not be equal, it does not deprive any individual in a society from having a means by which he can influence the political system through his share of power elements.

Since elite theory regards society as horizontally classified into a narrow, strong, influential minority as opposed to a vast non-organized majority that has no power, the majority is therefore subject to control by the elite. On the other hand, pluralism regards the society as classified on both a horizontal and a vertical bases. This societal classification induces a different vision of society as being composed of several competing groups. Elite theory believes in minority rule; pluralism believes mainly in majority rule.[3]

Both traditional and modern conceptualization of elite theory agree on the need to distinguish between the "elite" and the "masses" according to the possession of political power. Traditionalists hold that the masses are incapable of ruling themselves or are unwilling to. Thus, the existence of the elite is inevitable.[4] Modern elite theorists, on the other hand, emphasize that the elite uses the masses to gain sole possession of power. In this case, the existence of the elite is not inevitable, but is rather the result of the elite's capability to acquire all power sources in society i.e. wealth, authority, communications. and to control information in a direction that shapes public opinion in their favor.[5] The common denominator for explaining the existence of the elite, according to both groups of theorists, is the possession of power in society regardless of justification, reasons, or functions. Thus, all political systems can be divided into two categories: those who rule, and those who are ruled.

The first category is the "elite." It is the most crucial one for the political system as it holds the political power. By analyzing and understanding the characteristics of this category, the entire political system can be investigated.[6] Bottomore developed the concept of the counter-elite in an attempt to establish an implicit communication relationship between the elite theory and pluralism, i.e., between the minority and the majority theories.[7]

d. Different concepts—the same meaning. Elite theory has been built upon an assumption that there is always a controlling minority at the top of the political structure of the society. There are differences, however, over the definitions by which to describe this group, indicate its volume, detect its internal structures and components, investigate the sources of power, or define how this minority preserves its own continuity. This debate can be summarized as follows.

This ruling group has been variously identified as the elite, the ruling elite, the political elite, power elite, political class, and oligarchy.[8] A number of writers have addressed the internal structure of the elite. Michels points out that this small group always reaches the top of the ruling system and thus represents an oligarchy. Pareto, in turn, maintains that this elite group is divided into ruling and non-ruling elite since membership in the elite group does not automatically mean that an individual is a member of the ruling elite. An individual could be a member of an elite group which might be ruling or not according to the following measures: the superiority attained by using power to gain the acceptance of the ruled or the balance of power that exists among the various elite groups.[9]

Karl Deutsch[10] differentiates further between various elite groups by pointing out that the "elite" can be determined by using an official-post approach. Those who are believed to be "elite" are those who occupy strategic positions in the process of decision making, those who control the intersecting points of information flow, or those who participate daily in the making of decisions that effect millions of people.

Bottomore[11] also identifies three categories of elite: first the elite which represents the professional and functional group; second the political class involving all groups that practice power or political influence and those who are directly involved in the struggle for political leadership; and third the political elite which is a much smaller group of individuals who actually exercise their political power in society.

Different approaches have been developed to analyze the controlling group's sources of power.[12] Some refer to the personal characteristics of the members or, as Pareto calls them, the "residues" by which he substitutes personal attributes or factors (such as origins, or proximity to sources of power within the group) for the economic foundations of the ruling class as postulated by Marx. Mosca's approach concentrates on the organizational capability of the ruling class noting that that they are more able to articulate their interests and thus appropriate the key values of the society in the form of economic, military, or religion symbols. Michels considers that the source of power of the oligarchy lies within its intellectual supremacy and the personal characteristics of its members.

In explaining how the elite safeguard their positions and interests, most analysts agree that there is a constant necessity for them to work on stability and continuity.[13] Pareto considers that this goal is achieved through the process of elite circulation which includes two versions of power redistribution: internal and external. Internal circulation represents the capability of the elite to absorb ideas and individuals from outside the elite and integrate them within the elite so as to assure that no counter-elite is formed. External circulation is defined as circulation which occurs when the elite fail to achieve internal circulation and are thus replaced by anther, different elite group. Mosca points out that the stability of the elite rests on their ability to assemble a political equation that demonstrates their capacity to understand the dominant political formula in the society, and thereby control it. For example, in primitive society the military power was the key to societal status and superiority. In another society competition in using the religious symbols was more influential. In a third one, wealth or technology might be the ruling keys. Michels describes the process by which the elite maintains its existence and continuity as the *iron law of oligarchy*. He points to their ability to maintain stability and continuity by absorbing other individuals from outside the elite and integrating them within it (the same process that Pareto called internal circulation).

e. How to identify the elite and analyze it. If the elite is considered the appropriate approach to study the political phenomenon, we must consider two important dimensions: how do we identify the elite in the society? and what do we want to know about it? or how do we analyze it?[14]

With regard to the first dimension, the elite in any political society can be identified using several approaches. One approach is historical observation, which is advocated by both Mosca and Pareto, but is largely dependent upon the skills of the researcher and the sources available to him. Another is the official-post approach, wherein those who occupy certain official posts are considered to be the elite. A third is to regard anyone participating in political decision-making as a member of the elite. A fourth approach is the reputation approach in which those who have the reputation of being the elite are considered to be, in fact, elite.[15] Once the elite has been identified. the question then is: what do we want to know about this dominant group? Comparative politics literature emphasizes a number of essential determinants that should be considered when studying the elite:

1.) Social background, whether class, ethnicity, religion, regional, educational or professional background.
2.) Socio-political behavior of the elite—their adopted values in everything from political values through, for example, clothing.
3.) Elite's perspectives about themselves and the surrounding world, their orientations toward events and their interaction with them, which can be reliably determined by content analysis of the elite discourse.
4.) Personal characteristics of elite individuals determined by analyzing their individual behavior.

Potentialities of applying elite theory in the study of Arab political systems. The necessity of covalence and suitability between the theoretical and methodological framework and the phenomenon being research has been emphasized previously. The theory should focus on the fundamental aspects by which the phenomenon can be investigated, analyzed, and explained in a way that reveals its real nature without altering or reshaping the relative weights of its components.

Closer investigation of elite theory reveals that it focuses on important clues of political systems and suggests the most appropriate approach by which to understand and explain them. Focusing on the top of the political system provides specific potentialities for analysis that enable the researcher to understand phenomena the way they are. It also matches the basic nature of different elements of the intellectual and political realm, whether historical or contemporary.

The most essential potentialities that make the elite theory more appropriate for study of political systems are discussed here:

The nature of political societies is that authority cannot be exercised by everyone. There must be a small group of people administrating the affairs of a society whether in the most democratic or the most authoritarian systems. Even an authoritarian ruler needs a group of assistants through whom he can exercise wider control over the society. The existence of a small group of people controlling the major societal affairs is a well-known experience in human history and pervades all societies. The history of nations and peoples continuously highlights the presence of a minority that practices authority. Sometimes it seems that history goes forward through the interaction of relatively small groups of people who lead their nations and societies and determine their future.

A focus on the ruling minority has been characteristic of political thought since the early Greeks. The search has always been to determine who rules and the quality of the resultant political system, together with distinguishing between democratic and autocratic regimes.[16] This tradition has continued through modern times in most historical experiences or epistemological contexts, whether Western or Islamic. There has always been a common denominator in political thought represented by the intense focus and concentration on the top of the political system, considering it as the appropriate approach to understand, analyze, and reform in a given society.

The concept of state in the historical Arab Islamic experience means circulation and change, not stability and continuity. This concept of state has persisted through successive political eras and parallels the concept of elite, particularly in view of the fact that states or eras were identified with the names of families, dynasties, such as the Umayyeds, the Abbasids, the Iobeids, the Fatimids, etc.[17]

Further investigation of the contemporary Arab political reality reveals that there has been a continuity of the concept of the state as found in the Arab heritage. Such investigation of the nature of internal and external policies and their orientations clearly indicates that these policies were closely linked to the nature of the dominating elite. If the elite, in turn, reflect the personality of the political leader, the concept of state loses its stability and continuity and becomes linked, instead, with the concept of elite. The orientation of the state alternates from extreme left to extreme right and vice versa according to the nature of the elite and their orientation.

As previously noted, there is no history of well-defined rules for the political process in the contemporary Arab societies. This is the result of the lack of well-established democratic principles in the political practice and political life of the modern Arabs. Consequently, the political system in the Arab world has historically been dependent on the nature of the elite and thus has been subject to the internal transformation or alternation of these elite.

There are numerous potentialities for applying the elite theory to the understanding and analysis of contemporary Arab political systems. Arab reality has emphasized the importance of the role of the elite, and therefore, identifying and describing these elite would be a major means of understanding Arab political systems and the relevant political processes. If the class approach or group approach is attempted, it quickly becomes apparent that there are no well-defined class structures or groups in the Arab political systems as compared to Western political systems. The Western experience differs because its political problems result from the conflict of individual and group interests which forces both parties, individuals and groups, to integrate in political action through different political identities which they initiate according to the societal context. On the other hand, in African or Asian societies (which include the Arab countries) belonging to political groups don't play that essential role. Almond and Bowell reached this conclusion when analyzing comparatively both the African/ Asian experience and the Western one. This conclusion paves the way for an essential, axial role for the elite in the analysis of Arab political systems.[18]

Problematics encountered in the use of elite theory in studying Arab political systems. As stated, there are many potentialities for applying elite theory to the study of Arab political systems, but there are also many problems that could hinder this application or make the functionalization of this approach difficult, thus reducing its efficiency or effectiveness. The most important of these problematics are discussed as follows.

a. The disturbance of the relationships between the English term and the Arabic concept. This disturbance in the term-concept relationship can be illustrated in the translation of the English term "Elite" into the Arab word "*Nokhba.*" The disturbance results because the Arab word "*Nokhba*" means variously superiority, distinction, and ethical conduct. As many scholars assert that these admirable characteristics do not match the characteristics of most of the ruling Arab leaderships[19] it becomes apparent that the Arabic concept serves as a linkage between value and reality. Hence being an elite comes to be regarded as an advantage or a positive characteristic that gives a member of the elite a normative dimension that goes far beyond the mere concept as a tool for neutral scientific expression. Various circumstances surrounding the translation of the concept of elite into Arabic add further ambiguity to the already-ambiguous status of this concept in the Western context. The unstable condition between term and concept has two main sources: using various words to express the same meaning; and using the same word to express various meanings.[20]

b. The problematic of apparent conditions verses actual reality. Because there are no well-defined, obvious rules for the political process in Arab political systems, there has always been a problematic caused by the lack of correspondence between the apparent condition and the actual reality. As political eras progressed, and with each incident of transmission of power from one elite to another, diversities become more apparent—what has been believed to be true was not and the real truth was something else again. The heritage of each political system is always problematic and the answers are always wrong—those who were believed to be the real policy maker were not, etc.

c. The complexity and diversity of the foundation upon which the elite rests. If the power of the elite is expected to rest on residues, organizational capability or the ability to functionalize the political equation, the case of Arab political systems presents a different formulation. The base of the Arab elite differs from country to country, based on economic, cultural, ethnic, and religious factors. In some instances, the common base for Arab elite stems from association with certain educational institutions or with the military, or belonging to a certain political party, or on membership in an ethnicity, culture, or religion. In other cases all these factors play various roles in shaping the political elite.[21] In Syria, for example, the elite is based on the integration of ethnic, social, and religious factors representing family ties together with economic wealth. The continuity and stability of Syrian elite is achieved by widening the family ties to involve other principal social sources.[22] In Tunisia, the elite is based on several factors, i.e., association with certain modern educational institutions (whether in Tunisia itself or in France), belonging to the ruling Constitution Party, or being a close relative of the political leader.[23] In Egypt the elite are shaped by an interaction between family, friendship groups, and the patron-client relationship.[24] Thus the Egyptian elite is a mixture of heterogeneous components basically closed in its relations with the broader society, and is mainly dependent on the circulation of leading posts among its members to assure its continuity.[25] In Gulf states which are regarded as societies in the transitional phase of transforming from tribe into state,[26] the elite is very close to the framework of Ibn Khaldoun: *Asabiah* [social league] membership which is based upon social ties, whether *Asabiat Nasab* (family ethnic ties) or *Asabiat Intesaab* (political and social loyalties). Ibn Khaldoun's model related *Asabiyya* (social league) to a religious movement.He considered religion as the only source of legitimacy for the *asabiyya*, insisting that it could not justify itself without reference to a religious ideology. Saudi Arabia is the living example of Ibn khaldoun's model

d. The efficiency of vertical units in most of the Arab societies. When belonging to a tribe, region, or an ideology becomes an essential determinant in the structure and continuity of the elite, the elite as a whole belongs to the same tribe, region or political ideology. This situation is found in the Gulf States. When considering Yemen, Iraq, Syria, and other Arab countries no more details are needed to understand the very low efficiency of all horizontal units in those Arab societies.[27] The present-day reality is quite contradictory to the epistemological bases of elite theory that assumes that the horizontal classification of the society becomes the main and principal determinant of the political phenomenon.

e. The historical role of the state in making the elite. Throughout Arab history, politics more than any other factor played the main role in producing the elite. Holding political office, especially in the military or civil service, was considered as the only way to pass to the upper class or the elite. Modern Arab political systems are following the same socio-political formula with their elite being drawn from the same sources.[28]

f. The role of the political leader in establishing the elite and preserving it. Arab elite groups were established during different historical periods, and were dependent on the characteristics and personality of a certain political leader and his role. Thus the leader became the focus, point of reference, cause of being, and guarantee of continuity. Springburg calls this phenomenon the "patron-client" relationship.[29] He maintains that the study of elite and political systems should be approached by studying the political leadership, considering that the elite in this model is only a dependent variable that has no independent influence over the whole political system.

g. The co-existence between the elite and counter-elite. The co-existence of counter-elite groups means that restricting our analysis exclusively to the ruling elite will not lead to an understanding sufficient to explanation current political phenomena.

The nature of state-society relationship in contemporary Arab countries, and the continuing crises of the elite represented by a lack of credibility due to contradictory slogans and directives together with continuous failures in various areas have lead to a weakening of the trust between the elite and the people.[30] This results in undermining the legitimacy of most of these elite, causing the emergence of counter-elite that compete for legitimacy—either peacefully or violently.

h. Lack of data and information. One of the major problematics is the difficulty in acquiring appropriate and correct data concerning Arab elite and/or counter-elite. Thus, analyzing these elite groupings is correspondingly difficult. A factor in this difficulty is the secrecy that surrounds the elite combined with false information propagated about them.

A suggested plan for developing elite theory for the study of Arab political systems. It may seem elementary but it is nevertheless important to emphasize that theories cannot be judged to be true or false in themselves. They should be evaluated according to the extent to which they help or hinder the researcher in determining the truth. Theories should be viewed as more valid or less valid in terms of the phenomenon or subject being analyzed. It is also important to emphasize that theories of comparative politics do not necessarily compete with or contradict one another but can often be complementary and integratable. A researcher must understand the core of each theory and identify its postulates and hypotheses. He can then functionalize several individual theories. Thus, it becomes possible to develop a homogeneous methodological framework out of more than one theory, rather than restricting himself to a single theory, making it his only doctrine, and ignoring those dimensions which do not fit his analytical framework.[31] Accordingly, the study of Arab political systems suggests the use of a number of methodological tools that would increase the efficiency of elite theory by achieving full covalence between the theory and the phenomenon with which it deals, hence providing the theory with a validity and efficiency that enables understanding and explanation of the contemporary political Arab reality.

The general framework of elite theory—freed from the context and circumstances that accompanied its initial emergence—can be combined with some relevant concepts from the Arab cultural environment such as the idea of *Surrat*,[32] an Arabic term describing a group of people who are closely related to the society and who interact with it and with its social network in order to lead that society as guides or pioneers. The Khaldounian formula[33] of the concept of *Asabiah* can also be used in the sense that it does not restrict ethnic ties only to ethnic origin or family but also includes voluntary social relationships or alliances.

Elite theory can be functionalized within a comprehensive methodological package the framework of which is the system theory introduced by David Easton, the essence elite theory, and the primary tool the decision-making approach. With this triad, the political system can be more efficiently studied since system theory focuses on the elements of inputs and outputs, elite theory analyzes the external framework of the transformation process and the decision-making approach analyzes the internal framework of the entire process. Thus an integrated, comprehensive methodological package can be formulated with a graded arrangement of its components.

Elite theory can also be linked with the political economy approach that focuses on the economic backgrounds of the political phenomena.[34] The study of the social origins of the open-door policy elite in the Egyptian society conducted by Samia Said[35] is an example of this kind of linkage: elite theory and political economy. This linkage is apparent in Said's procedural definition of the elite as a combination of a traditional capitalist bureaucratic bourgeoisie and parasitic elements that come from a heterogeneous social matrix that possess substantial wealth, power, and influence ant is able it to exert pressure on all aspects of economic, political, and social life in Egypt in order to achieve its own interests and centralize the process of development. Said sketches the origins of the Egyptian elite and its connections that are, according to her, restricted to the traditional capitalist derivatives of the bureaucratic bourgeoisie and parasitic elements. She concludes that the traditional capitalist derivative is the real core of any capitalist formation in the Egyptian experience.

It is important to note that Said's use of a methodological combination involving both elite theory and political economy approach was an important methodological breakthrough, even though that methodological combination was unintentionally formed. Thus, the efficiency of operationalizing a methodological package proved capable of highlighting different aspects of the phenomenon being studied.

Linking elite theory and corporatism may be one of the most effective methodological tools yet developed for studying the Arab political system. This pattern of linkage can be regarded as relevant to the concept of "elite cartel"[36] within which the elite is considered as consisting of a group of pillars, that represent certain groups and aggregations of interest. The individual(s) located at the top of each pillar is considered a part of the elite and at the same time representative of that group of interests. Thus, the representatives of group attempt to accommodate their interests and those of the rest of the elite. Here, the elite is regarded as a group of representatives of the corporatist institutions of the society.[37]

In this sense, "corporatism" refers to Schimtter's definition of a system for interest representation where organizational units are arranged in the form of a number of different categories having a hierarchical organization and a coercive pattern of membership. These interest representatives are not competitive and are usually authorized or even established by the state. Hence, they have the right to manipulate the representation of the social groups that fall within their sphere in return for their participation in selecting the leaders and in organizing demands and support.[38] In the same context, the society is regarded as a group of corporatist organizations with the elite made up of representatives from the top of each "pillar."

By means of the foregoing methods, elite theory can be developed and operationalized more properly in the study of Arab political systems, so as to make the best use of this theory. The actual reality will be approached much more closely, and a larger number of its basic dimensions will be revealed. Thus, generally speaking, the evaluation of this phenomenon will be much richer and the results more valid. On the other hand, it is important to emphasize the need for re-testing and redeveloping the various theories after applying them in order to enrich each with diverse human experiences.

It is also necessary to increase the level of awareness of researchers as to the existing interactive relationships that involve all epistemological patterns. This interdisciplinary approach is particularly valid in today's intellectual climate since criticism and revisionism are currently dominant approaches that advocate reconsidering all of the major statements and hypotheses of social sciences and humanities as a way of representing post-modernity.

Notes

1. Arif, *The Re-enchantment of Political Science*, op. cit.
2. *Ibid.,*
3. Paolo Zannoni. *"The Concept of Elite," European Journal of Political Research*, vol. 6, 1978, pp. 16-17.
4. Robert A. Nye, *The Anti-democratic Source of Elite Theory: Pareto, Mosca and Michels* (London: Sage Publications, 1977).
5. Martin N. Marger. *Elites and Masses: An Introduction to Political Sociology*. New York: Van Nostrand,1991), pp. 78-79.
6. James Bill, and Robert L. Hardgrave. *Comparative Politics: The Quest for Theory. Columbus* (Ohio: Charles E. Merrill, 1973), pp.144.
7. George Lenczowski, ed., *Political Elite in the Middle East* (Washington DC: American Enterprise Institute for Public Research,1975), p.24.
8. Zannoni, op.cit.,pp.7-10
9. Ibid., pp. 15-16.
10. Karl Deutsch. *Politics and Government: How People Decide Their Fate* (Boston: Houghton Mifflin 1974), 2nd. Ed, pp. 48-52.
11. T.B. Bottomore. *Elites and Society* (New York: Basic Books, 1964), pp. 8-9. *See also* Lenczowski, op.cit., p. 6.
12. Chilcote, *Theories of Comparative Politics*, op.cit., p.351.
13. Ibid., pp. 359-351.
14. Lenczowski, op.cit., pp.1- 25.
15. Bill and Hardgrave, op.cit., pp. 165-167.
16. Richard L. Merritt. *Systematic Approach to Comparative Politics* (Chicago: Rand McNally, 1971), pp. 118-129.
17. Arif, *fi Musadir al-Turath al-Siyasi al-Islami*, op. cit., p. 87
18. Robert Springborg. *"Patterns of Association in the Egyptian Political Elite,"* in Lenczowski, op.cit., pp. 83-87.

19. Hariq, *al-Suratiyah wa al-Tahuwil al-Siyasi fi al-Mujtam' al-Arabi*, op. cit., p. 4
20. Zannoni, op.cit., p. 5.
21. P. A. Marr. *"Political Elite in Iraq,"* in Lenczowski, op.cit., pp. 109-149.
22. Elizabeth Bickarde, *"Naqad Mafhum al-Ithniyah fi Tahli al-Amaliyah al-Siyasiyah fi al-Watan al-Arabi,"* [Criticism of 'Ethnicity' Concept in Analyzing the Political Processes of the Arab World] in: Mosaad, ed., *al-Aalamiyah wa al-Khussusiyah fi Dirasat al Mantiqah al-Arabiyah*, op. cit., pp. 211-224
23. Hoda Hafez Mitkeis, *al-Nukhbah al-Siyasiyah fi Tunis, 1956-1970*, [Political Elite in Tunisia 1956-1970] (M.A. thesis, Cairo University, 1981), pp. 66-67.
24. Springborg, op.cit., pp. 93-104
25. Maisa al-Gamal, *al-Nukhbah al-Siyasiyah fi Misr*, [Political Elite in Egypt] *Al-Mustaqbal Al-Arabi*, Issue, no. 166, December 1992, pp. 50-53, *See also* Maisa al-Gamal, *al-Nukhbah al-Siyasiyah fi Misr: Dirasat Halat li-Majliss al-Wizaraa*, [Political Elite In Egypt: A Case Study of the Cabinet Elite] (Beirut: Markaz Dirasat al-Wihda al-Arabiyah, 1993), pp. 212-217.
26. Rida, op. cit., p.39.
27. Philip S. Khoury and Joseph Kostiner. *Tribes and State Formation in the Middle East* (Berkeley: University of California Press, 1990) See also Mohammed Hassan al-Zaahiry, *al-Dawur al-Siyasi lil-Qabilah fi al-Yaman 1962-1990*, [The Political Role of Tribe in Yemen 1962 – 1990] (Cairo: Madbuly Library, 1996).
28. About the role of the state in establishing the elite see: Michael Eppel,*"The Elite,The Effendiyya,and the growth of Nationalism and Pan-Arabism in Hashemite Iraq,1921-1958,"* *International Journal of Middle East Studies*,vol.30,no.2,May1998, pp227-247, John Davis, *Libyan Politics: Trib and Revolution* (London: Tours andCo.LIT,1987), pp.461-263, and Ehud R. Toledano, *"The Emergence of Ottoman-Local Elites 1700-1900:A Framework for Research,"* in: Ilan Pappe, and Moshe Ma'oz, *Middle Eastern Politics and Ideas : A History From Within*,(London: Touris Academic Studies,1997)
29. Springborg, op.cit., pp. 87-93.
30. Mahmud Mahammad al-Naku', *Azmat al-Nukhbah fi al-alam al-Arabi*, [Elite Crisis in the Arab World] (Published1989), p. 7.
31. Arif, *The Re-enchantment of Political Science*, op. cit.
32. Hariq, *al-Suratiyah wa al-Tahuwil al-Siyasi fi al-Mujtam' al-Arabi*, op. cit., p. 5. Hariq advocates using the concept of "Surrat" instead of the concept of "Elite" which he considered as a value-laden concept bearing western connotation. Hariq developed this "Surrat" concept out of a traditional Arab verse of poetry that states: People cannot do well in an anarchy without their leading "Surrat" who guide them. They will not be of any good and will have no chance if their "Surrat" were the ignorant ones who dominate and rule stupidly.
33. Ibn-Khaldun. *Muqaddemat Ibn-Khaldun* (Beirut: al-Aalamy Publications), pp. 135-136.

34. Arif, *The Re-enchantment of Political Science*, op. cit.

35. Samia Said Imam, *al-usul al-Ijtima'iyah li- Nukhbat al-Infitaah fi Misr 1974-1980*, [Social Origins of The Economic Open Door Policy Elite in Egyptian Society 1974-1980] (MA. thesis, Cairo University 1988)

36. Professor Martin Heisler used this concept "Elite Cartel" in a lecture at the University of Maryland, College Park, Md., USA, Summer 1992.

37. Douglas A. Chalmers, *"Corporatism and Comparative Politics"* in: Wiarda, ed., op. cit., pp58-80, and Lim A. Hammergren, *"Corporatism in Latin American Politics: a Reexamination of the Unique Tradition,"* *Comparative Politics*, vol.9, no.4 July,1977, pp.445-446

38. Ibid., pp. 445-446.

Chapter V

ℰↃᏇ

A Linguistic Approach to the Arab Politics: The Epistemological Connotation of the Arab Reconciliation

The importance of epistemological study of political issues and phenomena stem from the fact that studies of this kind concentrate mainly on transforming a particular question" into a "meta-question," by inquiring about the way this knowledge is produced and the way they highlight the questions or answer them.

Most of what we know, or claim to know was not studied in an epistemological way. By habits, we believe that we know all about that issue or that phenomenon without justifying our beliefs .We, usually don't really know whether these facts that we claim to know are true, or even whether we really know them for sure or not. The study of political phenomenon in the Arab world is no exception. Generally there are ideas or claims that become dominant without reflecting the actual reality; these ideas or claims don't express it, they don't accommodate with it. They themselves turn into a reality, an absolute, and a truth upon which other facts or truths are based or derived from. At this point, a comprehensive epistemological structure is erected without questioning any of its foundations. In cases where such an epistemological inquiry is carried out, other facts would come into purview or a modulation of the perceived facts would take place.

The base for this approach is the fact that "concepts" reflect the status of any cognitive field. They are theories in power. Since they are the nerves of theories and their actual foundation, they are the driving forces for any scientific field in its course. Analyzing a concept means analyzing the field itself because concepts are not words, they are "meanings," they reflect a point of reference and, they are groups of tools for collecting facts, besides, they are information containers.[1]

There is no such thing as unmediated study of facts including natural, social, and human phenomena. What we call facts are conceived, analyzed, and expressed through a system of nomenclature, which names their parts and components, and links the relationships of these parts and components. This nomenclature system uses these names, via concepts. Thus, concept is a name of a fact or a phenomenon by which it is identified and expressed. A concept should not only be linguistically considered, but also its factual significance should be included its linguistic meaning. Seen from this point of view the concept of **"reconciliation"** brings about epistemologically a condition of struggle among different parties whose common points are more than their disagreements. In this sense, a serious analysis of the interaction and cooperation of these groups becomes very important. Obviously, the interests of these parties are realized in various political, regional, and international frameworks. These conflicting parties will, in turn seek reconciliation as they realize the nature of their interests and how these interests would converge, coordinate, and correlate together. Thus, the interests of one party alone can't be achieved unless they are expressed and realized within a collective framework. Defining these interests requires them to be the real interests of the whole society not of groups, political elites, or any sort of narrow oligarchies.

In this sense, **"reform"** is a must in order to express the interests of those people as a real reflection of their actual interests. This essay will attempt to analyze these three interrelated concepts: **Reform, Interest,** and **Reconciliation,** by basing our analysis on an epistemological perspective that does not stop at the level of mere facts, but goes deeper into what we may call the "meta-being" of things, analyzing how these concepts were developed, and how these phenomena were brought into being. We shall see that in Arabic, these three concepts come from the same root-word *"salaha,"* and the linguistic connection between them is lost when translated into English. The essay takes up the challenge of epistemological skepticism in its present form and attempts to reconstruct the major theses proposed under a new light. The main purpose of the essay is to raise certain questions, rather than presenting ready-made answers or confirming certain facts. The seemingly positive language of the essay is nothing but a means to raise the question and the "meta-question." It is an invitation to rethinking the question and to reconsidering all that is passively perceived in the Arab intellectual life. We shall first ask why "Arab" reconciliation before asking "how." We attempt to answer the latter question based on an analysis of the inter-related concepts of reform *"islah,"* interest *"maslaha,"* and reconciliation *"musalaha."* It is only through such a critical outlook that we may come to grips with the actual reality of the Arab world.

Why Arab Reconciliation?

The historical context in which the call for Arab reconciliation emerged raises an essential question: Why does this reconciliation not involve Israel, Turkey, and Iran, as some of these states have gone into alliances with some Arab countries in the second Gulf War e.g. Turkey? Was it not true that some of these countries like Israel were attacked during this war the same way Kuwait was? Why should reconciliation be only amongst Arab countries while the consequences of the historical context makes them farther apart from each other comparing their existing relations with Israel, Turkey, or Iran?

The nature of this question or inquiry is generative as it calls for an epistemological framework to justify the nature of relations among Arabs and their interlacing ties that make them an independent entity and different from all other parties. Although the interests of some Arab states might intersect with some of the non-Arab states in the region in a certain historical moment or under some circumstances, this intersection remains at a superficial level not touching the crux of the matter. Hence, the former theme would raise another inquiry about the nature of these unifying Arab elements that make the Arab entity a social and civilizational being distinct from the surrounding countries. Despite the fact that some generative characteristics or political situations might exist to link that Arab entity with its surroundings,[2] This Arab entity might, as we define it here, leads us to an analysis of its components and foundations with an aim to clarify the contemporary Arab reality in a way that shakes the received categories and reconsiders the legitimacy of this issue. Some important points to be clarified in this context are the following:

1. The formation of this Arab entity is an epistemological one namely, it was not created out of a racist movement that sought unify the people of

a certain race within a nation-state the way it happened with Bismarck in Germany. This Arab entity was not developed as a result of a class revolution or a military coup, but it developed within an idea and a cognitive frame that was related to the emergence of Islam and the shift of the fragmented tribal loyalties of the Arabs into a liberating mission. This view thus included the "other" by going beyond the boundaries of race or ethnicity. This containment was achieved within a general framework based on unity through diversity. Therefore the Arab unity was based on a cultural integration that was established and presented by the Arab language together with the cultural frameworks that were relevant to Islam. These were the elements of this unity despite the fact that there were different states with different political frameworks, borders, passports, customs houses, and sovereignties. Moreover, this historical model was accompanied with an economic unity where markets were related and the exchange of goods was going on among all Arab countries. Thus, the cultural factors, then the economic dimensions, hence all the social activities formed strong bases for this unity. At the same time, these interrelations presented and supported the existence and continuity of that Arab entity in question.[3]

2. The Arab entity did not witness any sort of ruling regimes based on specific racist dogmas or fixed geographic boundaries. It was not a system imposed by the winner over the looser. It was not a racist system compared to the racist meaning of nationalism but emerged as a system polarizing the peoples' loyalty and attracting them to its norms because it gave them more civil freedoms in addition to the economic, social, religious freedoms they gained under its rule. Elements of flexibility were present in that system in a vital interaction with the traditional patterns of the people of these areas where they have developed themselves.[4]

3. Arab history did not develop the modern concept of "state" which means the stability, rigidity, continuity, and sovereignty of certain people over a region under a certain political administration. On the contrary, the Arab conception of state historically meant the circulation of the ruling elites, the ruling power, with expanding or narrowing domains of the region, and with the increase or decrease of the number of the ruled people. That's why the notion of "state" refers to the ruling regimes or political eras, Hence we have the Umayyads, the Abbassids, the Tolonians, the Akhshidians, theAyyubids, the Fatimids, the Murabitun, the Muwahideens, the Mamlouks, or the Ottomans states.

Capital cities were numerous as the center of the state was shifting from one region to another without having the contemporary significance of centralism. There were no states or sub-entities polarizing the loyalty of the people with the perception of an invader. Yet there were different political formulas that are quite apart from that we know now or those known at the time of old empires.[5]

4. The fragmentation of the Arab entity after the World War II didn't originate from the will of the people. Those nation- states were not formulated on their own to reflect the structural characteristics of their people. They were formed on the basis of the treaties and agreements among European parties,[6] As we see, these Arab nation-states were not the expression of the will of their own people but of a counter -will that was imposed over them by colonialism which divided the region according to the interests, biases, and future aims of colonial powers. The result of this was the following:

The boundaries imposed by colonialism do not match the social, cultural, or ethnic characteristics of Arab states that are known as part of stable and continuing civilizations such as Egypt, Iraq, and Syria. The inhabitants on the sides of these states borders represent deep linkages and connections between Arab states because they do not belong to that state or the other as there is not specific historical, cultural, and social entity of one of these states totally different from the other.

Because the borders were not erected between these Arab states on natural bases reflecting the geographic historical or social reality, the border problems were the most important ones in the Arab world. The border conflicts were the main origin of most of the conflicts in the region.[7]

The legitimacy of these fragmented nation-states has always been under doubt and skepticism. The full legitimacy of a state was never established even though the existing political systems gained some sort of legitimacy. Hence the call for an Arab, an Islamic, or a regional unity has always expressed an imminent rejection of the legitimacy of the nation state. The border claims between one state and another also has been a serious impediment for the legitimacy of this regional state condition. This in turn has led to the explosion of numerous border conflicts to the extent that no Arab State is free from having regional demands towards one or more of its neighbors.

5. What is the historical point of reference for the contemporary Arab states? The former analysis suggests that questioning the historical point of reference becomes a must in this context. If historical justifications are skipped over together with the continuos attempts to fragment Arab history in order to match it with the history of these nation states. Then the ultimate question is where the history of Qatar, Bahrain, Kuwait, Saudi Arabia,

Lebanon, Jordan, or Libya starts, considering boundaries that they have at the moment. Where does the history of Tunisia or Algeria start with the existing international borders at the moment? No answer was found for these questions before World War I or after the World War II in some cases. In this sense, it is important to distinguish between a regional entity called Algeria and the drawing of a national border in a very artificial way even as we see in the case of Egypt, Iraq, or Syria. Such historical/ civilizational identities existed before but they lacked a historical point of reference in its contemporary form. The case of Egypt raises the important question: does the Nile valley or the Nail valley with *al-Sham* and *al-Hejaz* and a part of Libya and Sudan represent Egypt? Thus the name Egypt is used to signify a mobile phenomenon in the sphere of a larger entity where no social or civilizational departure existed between the different components.

Political independence has existed at some stages of this history as the local ruler continued to rule in some independent ways. Nevertheless the lack of historical legitimacy of these sub-units of Arab entity has to led to the crisis of geographical legitimacy because they were determined by treaties and agreements among European powers and the Ottoman empire during its last phase.

In this sense, it can be concluded that the geographical legitimacy of the existing borders drawn under these circumstances is in crisis. This however, does not mean that only some Arab states lose their legitimacy in relation with other states but rather all the Arab states share this legitimacy crisis. The lack of historical legitimacy in relation with "*ummah*" as a historical being can not be an excuse used by any Arab state against the other as we see in the case of Iraq and Kuwait.

To sum up, we can say that the artificial determination of the historical point of reference in dealing with the problematic of Arab reality is an issue that needs revision and reconsideration.

Arab Reconciliation: How?

Considering the divided nature of the Arab world, one expects, from time to time, some conflicts that emanate from the very condition of this political unit in question. Although the Arab stakes seem to have some sort of legitimacy within the existing international order, they lake, or we have seen, any serious basis for a strong political structure. An entity like the Arab political structure cannot consider reconciliation among its units with a pragmatic perspective or a temporary situation. What is needed is a fundamental transformation of structural relations with all that such a transformation implies. This, in turn, requires the relinquishment of formalist categories of political and diplomatic values that determine current politics. Achieving this reconciliation also requires establishing an interest-motivated base for the Arab entity as a whole involving all of its component units on the one hand and its conflicting parties on the other. Formulating these interests on various levels necessitates the start of a genuine accommodation process between the interests of the Arab entity as a whole and the definite interests of its units. As none of each should dominate the other or else the solution will be a temporary one, a false promise that would erupt in more violently later on. Unless such a pre-condition is provided, interests will be not the interest of the whole of the organizing institution of this Arab entity with its mechanisms and tools that represent the political willing of the sub-units without reflecting the real collective interests of the whole Arab world.

At this juncture, it is important to note that "reform" at the level of the ruling regimes of the Arab world is a must to regain their legitimacy so as to become accepted by their own people. It is the only way by which the goals and the interests of these people are reached in a rational way. Reform is a must also at the level of collective identity of the Arab world in order to strike a balance between the interests of the individual members of the Arab world and those of the entire structure. It is only through such balance that the myth of eroding the system from inside in order to achieve one's owns interest can be dispelled. Certain organizational and institutional frameworks however should be established to carry out this mission. In this regard, the necessary steps required to develop a consistent discourse about Arab reconciliation will be based on solving the structural crisis of the Arab system, not the superficial manifestations of it. They will also be based on achieving balanced interests in order to make it a more comprehensive and truthful one.

These three concepts **"Reform,"** **"Interest,"** and **"Reconciliation"** come from the same root in Arabic and the linguistic connection is lost when translated into English. In Arabic they all come from the root-word *"Salaha"* meaning the abolishment of all evil, and the return of things back to their natural status of well-being which is *"Salah"* i.e. correctness or well-being.

Reform" *Islah"* is the contrary of deform, meaning to correct deformities, to maintain the pristine form of things, and to return them back to their natural style. Interest *"Maslaha"* is against damage, loss, or corruption. Reconciliation *"Msalaha"* means regaining the natural warm relations among the different parties. Thus, all these words share the same significance in

Arabic, which is confronting corruption and deformities so as neutralize them.[8] hence, the unified significance of these terms signifies the correlation and interlacement among their meanings. In this sense, we can give a coherent statement stating that **reconciliation** requires **reform** to achieve the **interests**.

Before going further into the details of these concepts or the three phases they represent, it is important to emphasize a number of elementary issues which include:

a) Both concepts of **reform** and **interest** can be reinterpreted within different ideologies and intellectual trends. Hence, dealing with these concepts in the context of this research will be limited to the epistemological and methodological dimensions only without favoring a particular theory of reform or interest.

b) The pattern of dealing with these two concepts should be continuously questioned and revised in order to reach an optimal formula to actualize both of them in a way that will reflect the reality of Arab society and its great diversity. This diversity should not be ignored or abused. On the contrary, it should be dealt with by preserving the Arab identity while at the same time maintaining its cultural and moral values.

c) These two concepts will be dealt with within three successive levels including: the cultural structure of Arab masses with specific concentration on the intellectual class; the nature of the relationship between the ruler and the ruled or between the state and the society; and the nature of relationships among political systems within the activities of the "Common Arab Act."

Reform "*Islah*":

The concept of "reform" is the heart of many theories in political science to be found at every level of political literature. In some cases, it is described as a process of "change" but generally it is seen as the structural rebuilding of apolitical system. In all cases, the concept implies the necessity of erasing errors and deformities with their different elements and causes. It signifies the process of returning things back to their spontaneous natural course; in order to allow the various political phenomena to develop properly and correctly, and reflect their influence in their own way within their own context by means of a voluntary process of change that aims at erasing the obstacles, deformities, and corruption mechanisms; so as to open the way for the opposite mechanisms that lead to progress and development. Approaches to "change" are quite numerous and different. There are political approaches together with economic and social ones. In all these approaches, change is induced by the enhancement of behavior and action in the way that alters the perception of knowledge and the way of interpreting reality. According to this theme, change will be determined and its mechanisms will be specified according to the level of awareness of a particular society and its potential response to change. Human knowledge and perception develops firstly at the level of the ideas, then at the level of beliefs. Hence, the relationship between "knowledge" and "behavior" becomes deeper and more spontaneous whenever the level of perception is high. Therefor, inducing change in such conditions will be more difficult requiring more time and effort. On the contrary, behavior related to simple ideas is easier to change than the one arising from stable solid conceptions. On the other hand, behavior related to holistic beliefs is the most difficult one to change. It might be better to leave it as it is without attempting to change any of its themes as the Quranic notion states: "You have your own religion and I have mine."[9]

Any possible/plausible program of change compasses the following stages:

The Level of Epistemological Cultural Structure:

The level of cultural structure is the most important one upon which the variables and dimensions of change are based. The change in perceptions, concepts, and ways of thinking is quite essential to induce reform in the Arab reality. The nature of the first Arab entity was linked either with a socialization process that has concentrated on cultural change,[10] it therefore became a social rule which states that "God would not change people unless they change themselves."[11] Among the cognitive determinants to be considered in studying the Arab cultural structure, the following points should be noted :

1. There is an apparent domination of the philosophy of poetry over the methodology of Arab thinking in general. As the Arab culture was formed at most of its stages within the perception of poetry as the main creative and communicative tool of culture and as the principal form of interaction between pure reason and absolute spirit. Hence, this cultural structure gave rise to a specific mentality that contradicts with the scientific mentality in most of its dimensions. The poet creates his own reality i.e. the one that he wants instead of accepting what is really the case. In Arab culture, poetry has always been an attempt to establish a new vision of life that differs in its components and relationships from the actual one people live. This is a

style much easier than understanding the actual reality and accepting to deal with it the way it is. In contrast to this, science is a discipline based on facts and it attempts to approach the truth by means of these facts only.

As a conclusion of the former analysis, most of the contemporary Arab intellectuals in general are nothing but a "poet" who uses the language and terminology of science in search of the creation of a reality of his own. Moreover, he attempts to create history extensions derived out of this executive reality of his in a way that gives him a historical point of reference. So, the end result of this situation would be nothing but losing the remaining available ground of intellectual dialogue. Which was supposed to be the base for reaching some common rules and highlighting certain common dominators that already exist in the Arab reality that would push Arab ties and Arab interests forwards.

2. Dualism in thought and practice is one of the characteristics of the Arab intellectual life today. The Arab intellectual is mostly an one-sided when it comes to his epistemological orientations. In this sense, he perceives matters in a binary way as if there is nothing but the two edges of an extreme continuum; i.e. it is either "tradition" or "modernity," "originality" or "contemporarism," "nationalism" or "Islam," "conservatism" or "revolutionism," etc. Within these dualisms, the energy of the contemporary Arab intellectuals is consumed and wasted. Dualism serves as a vast gate for internal conflicts that divide the Arab nation into sects and tribes who fight each other. The end result is a dramatic fragmentation of the Arab entity and Arab efforts creating iron partitions and deep trenches that hinder the communication, interaction, and unification of the Arab world.

3. Extremism and absolutism are the basic ways by which the Arab intelligentsia perceives all matters whether they are of an absolute or relative nature. The Arab intellectual often speaks for the masses (all the masses). He always claims to grasp the ultimate truth leaving no space for reconsideration. Each group of people, each party, or intellectual tribe believes that it possesses the whole truth and no one else could know anything about it. In this closed intellectual context, whoever has a different point of view, opinion, or idea he is labeled as traitor, ignorant, regressive, conservative, infidel, or any of these classifications and descriptions.

4. The weakness of the intellectual class in the Arab world, whether at the level of the demolishing existence of this class, the direct action it develops, or the role it performs, is perceived as the final result of the binary oppositions that have fragmented that class into different trends and ideologies. Marred by this bind of intellectual tribalism, the Arab

intelligentsia can never come to grips with the current problems of its world, not even the most elementary ones. Thus, this intellectual crisis becomes a prominent factor in deepening the fragmentation of the Arab intellectual class.[12] In addition to this, a vast status of dependency is easily noted in most of the activities of this intellectual class. It is an unbalanced dependency on the ruling regimes, which is not limited to advising the ruler, but goes as far as justifying the existence of that ruling regime in spite of its inefficiency. The end result is that this intellectual class becomes a tool used by the regime to re-shape the awareness of the masses in order to direct their orientations into certain trends that would not be in their favor or in the favor of the nation as a whole. As for the dependency on the external powers or institutions, it is to be noted that the Arab intellectual class, when caught up this sort of dependency, end up by fulfilling and preserving the interests of those external powers at the expense of the interests of the Arab nation.[13]

Relationship Between the Ruler and the Ruled:

This level is one of the most sensitive ones in dealing with the issues of Arab society. It should be deeply examined, and well considered as it is the real reason of all crises of the Arab entity at its different historical stages,[14] this level of political relationship witnesses plenty of crises which in turn generate visible and invisible consequences on various levels of the Arab world, thus, influencing the sub-components of the Arab system. The main problematics of this level of relationship can be summed up as follows:

1. The rupture between the ideology of the elite and the culture of society is a very prominent feature of the contemporary Arab society. The Arab intellectual elite in general refers to the ruler and those who function in the field of power practice as culture makers, industry makers, traders, bureaucrats, or military commanders. Those elite members do have a certain modern culture whose point of reference is nothing but a heterogeneous mixture of traditional and modern cultures. The modern component often represents some imminent epistemological origins of foreign languages and foreign cultures, which the ordinary Arab citizen can not communicate with. So, the Arab masses remain bound to the Arab-Islamic culture which was formulated through the historical interaction between Islam as an epistemological source and the cultural frameworks of the hereditary perceptions of the Arab people which have developed and interacted with Islam creating a unique cultural pattern. This cultural identity of the Arab masses is quite different or even contradictory to the ideology of the ruling

regimes and the cultural orientations of the intellectual elite. This deep epistemological rupture diminishes the efficiency of the Arab system as a whole and leads to the stagnation of the entire society. As a result, it becomes impossible to mobilize the Arab society. All the eminent abortive factors that were present in the successive Arab renaissance projects start to function at this level. The overall meaning of this condition is that each revival project has its own elements of collapse and failure embodied within its original structure.

2. The rupture between the ruler and the ruled is found because of the absence of strong traditions of governing that might have established a channel of communication between these two parties. In this sense, if such traditions had existed, the participation of the ruled would have become a genuine component of the structure of the Arab political system and its activities. Rulers in turn will be seen as normal as human beings not gods or semi-gods. It is only through the 'normalization' of politics, so to speak, that we can hope for a mere reasonable and humane form of governance in the Arab world.

3. According to the forgoing analysis, the problem of legitimacy is quite apparent in the Arab world. It wouldn't make sense to say that this Arab regime or that possesses enough legitimacy arising from the voluntary acceptance of its citizens.[15] There are plenty of legitimacy sources that are mostly outside the will of the people. Sometimes it is a historical legitimacy gained in a hereditary way or in a certain historical phase, in other cases it is a revolutionary, tribal, ethnic, religious, or family legitimacy. In all these modes of Arab legitimacy, the presence or the mere existence of the people is denied or ignored.

4. As result of ignoring the fact that people represent an important source of legitimacy, a new source of legitimacy come upon the scene in the Arab world. It is the legitimacy created outside the whole Arab sphere; it is either the international legitimacy or that of the super powers, the international institutions, or the international public opinion. The satisfaction and appreciation of these international powers is being perceived, at the moment, as the main source of actual legitimacy of most of the present Arab regimes. Sometimes the legitimacy and creditability of knowledge itself becomes based on that foreign source even if the living experience proved otherwise. Those who are described, as human rights violators or terrorism sponsors are automatically believed to be so regardless of any critical investigation. Even the most elementary facts of the Arab world is subjected to the legitimatization process of foreign discourses. Accordingly, Israel would

be a peaceful state having no nuclear weapons or weapons of mass destruction because the international legitimacy believes so, while Iraq whose forces and powers are totally destroyed is believed to have such weapons!

5. the inability to mobilize and inspire the people towards a specific major goal is one of the characteristics of the Arab system because these ruling regimes do not hold any supreme national goals or grand projects. Such national goals or major projects are turned into an instrument of conflicts among the Arab states. They are also being used as a justification for the legitimacy of certain Arab regimes that lack deeply any sort of grass roots support. To give an example, the Palestinian issue was turned into a major Arab problematic and an arena for Arab conflicts instead of being a supreme national cause that would mobilize all the Arab towards a common cause.[16]

The Level of Interaction Among the Different Units of the Arab Entity:

A number of terms should be available to start with reconstructing an Arab regional system. These terms or conditions can be considered as the pillars for reforming the pattern of interaction among the different units and parties of the Arab entity.[17]

1. Achieving harmony and homogeneity among the interactive components of the Arab entity, together with harmonizing the concerns of the Arab societies, so as to make the issues and interests of Arab policies a truthful reflection of the interests and concerns of the Arab people. In this sense, the interests and concerns of a specific Arab state or a particular Arab region would not dominate over those of the whole Arab world. So, there will be no particular party determining the agenda of the Arab world and shaping it according to its own interests.[18]

2. Establishing a number of standards, values, and general rules that governs the interactions among the different components of this Arab entity. Regardless of the source of these general-governing values, they should be accepted and obeyed by all Arab parties. In this sense, a certain control over the Arab will be imposed so as none of the interactive processes can go beyond the limits that preserve the stability, integrity, and unity of the Arab entity as a whole.[19]

3. Achieving independence at the international level is a crucial task for the Arab world at the moment. If it was assumed that any Arab regional order should achieve a certain level of independence from the major

international powers and institutions that influence the international arena,[20] the Arab entity cannot remain neutral or self content having a clear conscious regarding this matter. The geographical position, historical evolution, and civilizational role of the Arab world confirm all together the inevitable necessity of formulating an independent Arab strategy to deal with this situation. It has been the lesson of history that the Arab entity has no choice but being a vital actor in the region responding to the strategic realm that surrounds it. If such Arab action was not taken, the Arab world would be subjected to the influence of other powers. Hence, it will be subjected to either civilian occupation or dependency. This is, however, not to suggest that the generative origin of this situation has any thing to do with the Arab religious relations with the West. Since the beginning of the struggle of the Persian, and Roman empires, certain geo-strategic considerations induced most of the confrontations between the East and the West up to our own day.[21]

Furthermore, the mere existence and continuity of this Arab entity required developing its role and pursuing an independent project so as to polarize all the efforts of the Arab sub-units to put them on the way to independence at the international level. This process should be carried out within a comprehensive perception of the Arab entity's potentialities and capabilities, together with the limitations of international maneuvers and the nature of the dominant international order. Two examples can be given to illustrate this point: Nasser of Egypt and King Faisal of Saudi Arabia. Both of them could manage to develop a role for the Arab world

4. The development of the institutional frameworks that are necessary for enhancing the efficiency of the Arab entity is another requirement for vitalizing the Arab role. If the existing Arab league were to achieve a degree of efficiency not at the level of realizing its political goals but at the level of requiring a degree of acceptability by its members. This would make all the parties interested in participating into its institutions and having some sort of coordination among themselves.[22]The recent developments specially after the second Gulf crisis has led to more erosion of this symbolic function of the Arab league. Therefore, the weakened role of the Arab League resulted in more dramatic and crucial consequences that become even clearer in its total absence from the scene in cases of Somalia and Yemen. Also, the Arab league was completely ignored during the second Iraqi-Kuwaiti crisis in October 1994.

In this sense, the notion of developing Arab institutions to achieve a certain degree of enforcement for the Arab entity must overcome the present existing frameworks. And the way to do this is not to abolish them completely but by blowing a new spirit into them. If the Arab League, which is seen as the sick man of the east who inherited the role of the Ottoman empire, is supposed to represent the nodal nexus of Arab sovereignties, then more institutions should be established besides this League in order to strengthen the Arab entity and benefit from the experiences of the European union. This open use of the European experience must be done to achieve coordination and covalent presentation of the Arab states sovereignties, other Arab institution should be established and developed to deal directly with the people the way the European court for human rights does in order to avoid the cracks that became quite apparent in the Arab entity on the social level.

Another important step to be taken is to create new institutions and organizations that will operate at the level of various Arab states such as the union of Arab lawyers and the like.. These are the most important determinants of the reform process to be carried out in accordance with the realities of the Arab word. This, in turn, will be succeeded by a wider program at establishing and maintaining a comprehensive Arab reconciliation based on mutual respect, values, and on belonging to a polity that overcomes the ethnicity-based considerations and contemporary tribalism. This was the way the Pre-Islamic Arabs were transformed from barbarian tribes into a civilizational entity at the hand of Islam. As Plato says: "The real reform is achieved by a total reform that guarantees reforming the justice politics together with reforming the concepts of virtue, pleasure, beauty, and art." So, freedom and unity to create in turn the individual in an integrated society must complement this reform. This reform would confront and hopefully diminish corruption that leads to slavery and conflict. Reform is a matter of change that should be calculated within a time equation.[23] A simple gradual change will lead in time to the required end results. Yet, it should have a starting point that pushes change forward in the required direction. Finally, reform must be an integrated comprehensive process.

Interest *"Maslaha"*:

Reform at various levels is a necessary condition to achieve the interests of the Arab people. There is no epistemological proof within the context of the existing Arab reality that would prove that the interest of a certain Arab nation-state or the whole Arab entity is the real and basic interest of the people. Determining the real interests of Arab people is an extremely difficult task because the question of representation, i.e., who will represent the interests of Arab peoples is a very complicated question. An illusive interest is usually adopted, together with personal, sectarian, elitist, or ideological interests. It is not a weak possibility that the interests of foreign powers might be adopted by those who are supposed to seek the Arab interest. Such foreign interests are quite liable to go on the contrary with the Arab nations' interests conflicting with most of the interest of the Arab nation-states or the Arab entity as a whole.

Interests are considered by some people as the elementary idea of the science of politics. Polity is sometimes defined as the sphere within which interests compete to gain the admission of their existence and realization.[24]

There is a distinction between two main views in contemporary politics on the question of defining interests:

The first view is the subjective one, which places the determination of interest within people's feelings, orientations, wishes, and demands. In this sense, interests express a general feeling or orientation towards some thing or issues that are identified as interests.

The second view is the descriptive or objective one, which does not count on feelings, orientation, or demands. Yet, it regards interests as means to satisfy the various requirements or as those means that would lead to happiness.[25]

"Interest" means utility and profit. So it is against incorrectness or corruption. It is to be defined as "pleasure" as Abu Hamid al-Ghazali describes "interest" as bringing profit and preventing harm. In this sense, "interest" is defined as goodness or well being. Most worldly interests are defined by "reason" so no reasonable person is incapable of identifying the mere interests or the mere disadvantages of people. Yet, the existence of both interests and counter-interests in separate forms is rare because most worldly matters are mixed with interests and counter-interests.[26] Therefore, the existence of an absolute measure by which the quality of interests is measured is a must. Identifying the interests of the Arab entity must be carried out on certain levels that should go in parallel with complete coordination and harmony. On these levels the interests of the political Arab groups is to be identified in each state separately and the interests of the whole Arab entity is to be identified as a whole. At the same time, the coordination of both state interests and the interests of the whole Arab entity must be met without contradictions and without sacrificing a certain state's interests for the sake of the others.

Arab national security is one of the most crucial macro-interests of the Arab world as it should be regarded as a holistic integrated totality that can not be achieved for a certain state at the expense of the whole Arab national security.

The issue of security can never be analyzed from a restricted point of view. The integration and interlacement of security interests of all Arab states is not a voluntary matter that can be accepted by some Arabs and denied by others. It is a given situation where external threats and dangers on all geo-strategic, social, and civilizational levels are spontaneously erupting one after the other. Thus, no claim of full control over these threats or dangers may be given any sort of credibility. The contemporary Islamic movement is a very clear example for such threats. It has the same character which the Nasserist, Pan Arabist, and Arab nationalist movements had before. So, it can be concluded that the strategic dangers and threats do have the same course.

Furthermore, defining the state's interests or the collective ones of the Arab entity requires highlighting the mutual interests that gather all the Arabs. For example, those interests that arise from building up deep and strong interactions among the Arab countries within the context of an international order that does not allow the existence of any small fragmented entities giving no legitimacy to those who do not join a major global bloc. Because such blocs are being established on different levels in the contemporary global scene, an Arab bloc becomes a must in this context.

Thus, having these strong and vital interactions among the Arabs would bring about a common ground for the realization of Arab interests and highlight other interests that have been ignored or marginalized so far.

3. Reconciliation *"Musalaha"*:

By achieving reform and defining the real interests of Arab countries we can start dealing with the issue of reconciliation that should be achieved in order to handle the roots of the problems and challenges facing the Arab world. This reconciliation should be based on realization of the nature of the Arab national and moral interests and the complexity of the present Arab situation. It should also admit the essential needs and necessities that govern the strategic orientations of the Arab countries. This admission will be a vital step to search for coordination between these needs and necessities in the way that guarantees the well being of the Arab nation as a whole.[27]

The previous experiences of the Arab reconciliation and dispute settlement have shown to be insufficient and inactive. These reconciliation attempts were only calming down the conflicting situations or imposing certain settlements that were the only alternative available due to the extraordinary circumstances. These settlements never touched the heart-core of any Arab-Arab conflicts. Hence, their effect have always been temporary and quickly vanishing, thus, giving the cycle of conflict another turn.

The recurrence of Arab conflicts has always been a dramatic characteristic of Arab-Arab relations because all reconciliation attempts were nothing but a hasty way of putting a thin layer of new painting over an older one to hide the ugly features of the old system. Anyhow, these hidden features start to appear because that thin layer diminishes as time goes by.[28] The most frightening thing about Arab disputes and conflicts is that the traditional factors of reconciliation have been loosing their effect since 1981. This means a much darker future for the notion of "Arab Solidarity."[29]

Of course, these new findings require overcoming the collateral factors of cooling off the conflicting situation in search of new methods that would lead to developing some radical solutions to all crises of the Arab world by making use of the previous experience. If these solutions are not introduced, the cycle of attempt and failure will go on forever. If these radical solutions are not fulfilled, the Arab memory will recall the failure of the Arab system as it lacks the proper realization of the threatening dangers that might induce full fragmentation of the Arab world and full collapse of the Arab system. This condition is expected to take place because of the ignorance of the present political situation whose real sources and origins must be detected. It is a fact that ignoring the living political situation and its conflicts, the wrong estimation of the basic interests that link all Arab countries, underestimating the dangers that arise from the fragmented Arab situation,[30] together with depending on the change of the ruling regimes as the only mean to solve the Arab-Arab conflicts, represent in general the most essential reasons for the failure of the Arabs in overcoming their conflicts. The subjective nature of relationships among the Arab rulers is one of the largest failures of the Arab entity in soking its conflicts.

As mentioned before, depending on the change of the rulers as a final solution of most of the Arab-Arab conflicts is a sort of mental image that reduces all matters to the level of personal relations. If the anemic Arab ruler vanishes or is replaced, the door becomes open for the interference of other Arab countries in the internal affairs of this ruler's country to induce a change in the political system, thus, abolishing the essential factors of the conflict.[31] The personal subjective dimensions of the problematic are always highlighted as the conflict remains within the mind of the political decision maker rather than at the objective level.[32] The examples for this situation are numerous such as the Egyptian-Libyan conflict during the era of the president Sadat or the Sudanese-Egyptian conflict during the era of Mubarak. These conflicts are based only on political decision making, yet, they have no roots at the level of the empirical actual aspects. The final conclusion is that the process of reconciliation should be defined as the interaction between two or more parties that have a full and deep realization of the necessity of such reconciliation together with the severity of the situation. In this sense, reconciliation will be achieved not by the sentimental/emotional feelings to gain certain political goals or even to break the stagnant Arab reality. On the contrary, reconciliation will be based on the notion of realizing the supreme Arab interests within the present world order. In this sense, the apparent or imminent threatening factors shall be well perceived by the whole Arab entity, thus, rationally confronted on the bases of the strategic Arab interests.

Notes

1. Zannoni, op. cit.,pp.1-5, and Giovanni Sartori, *"Concept Misformation in Comparative Politics,"* *The American Political Science Review*, vol. 64, no. 4, December 1970, p.1052

2. Abul-Fadl, *Madkhal Minhaji li-Dirasat al-Nuzum al-Siyasiyah al-Arabiyah*, op.cit., pp.5-7.

3. Tirbin, op. cit., pp.21-23.

4. Ibid., p. 21

5. Abul-Fadl, *Madkhal Minhaji li-Dirasat al-Nuzum al-Siyasiyah al-Arabiyah*, op.cit., pp. 96-103

6. Tirbin, op.cit.,p.13, and Munir Shafiq, *al-Islam wa Tahadiyat al-Inhitat al-Mu'asr: Qadaiya al-Tajziyah, wa al-Suhuniyah, wa al-Tagtiyb*, [Islam and the Challenges of Contemporary Decadence: Issues of Fragmentation , Zionism , and Westernization] (Cairo , al-Zahraa lil-I'lam al-Arabi, 1987), pp. 117-128.

7. Ahmad Yusuf Ahmad, *"al-Nizam al-Dawli wa Azmat al-Khalij"* [The International Order and Gulf Crisis] in: Ahmad al-Rashiydi, ed., *al-Ina`kasat al-Dawliyah wa al-Iqliymiyah li-Azmat al-Khalij*, [Regional and International Implications of the Gulf Crisis] (Cairo: Markaz al Buhuth wa al-Dirasat al-Siyasiyah bi-Jama'at al-Qahirah, 1991), pp.214

8. Ibn-Manzour: *Lessan al-Arab* [The tongue of the Arabs: a lexical language book], (Cairo: Dar al-Maarif, 1979),p. 2479.

9. Ali Gumaa Muhammad, *"Falsafat al-Tagiyr,"* [Philosophy of Change], in: *Nadwat Manahij al-Tagiyr fi al-Fikr al-Islami*, [The Methodologies Change in Islamic Thought Seminar], Ministry of Awqaf, Kuwait , 24-26th Jan. 1994, pp.11-12 , and *The Qura'n*,109:6

10. Mona Abul-Fadl, *al-Umah al-Qutub*, [The Pole-Nation] , (Cairo: 1982), pp. 73-80.

11. *The Qura'n*, al-Ra'd,13:11

12. Saif al-Deen Ismai'l, "*Harb al-Kalimat fi Harb al-Khalij: Azmat al-I'lam wa I'lam al-azmah*," [Words War in Gulf Problem: The Crisis of the Media and the Media of Crisis] in: Mustafa Kamil aL-Saiyd, ed., *Hatah la Tansha` Harb Arabiyah-Arabiyah Ukhra: Min Duruss Harb al-Khalij*, [To Prevent Arab-Arab War to Erupt: Lesson of Gulf War] (Cairo: Markaz al Buhuth wa al-Dirasat al-Siyasiyah bi-Jama'at al-Qahirah, 1991), pp.197-244

13. Hamid Rabai', *al-Thaqafa al-Arabiyah bina al-Gazwu al-Sihuni wa Iradat al-Takamul al-qawmi*, [Arab Culture between Zionist Invasion and National Will for Integration, (Cairo: Dar al-Mawkif al-Arabi, 1983), pp.137-180.

14. Saif al-Deen Ismai'l, *al-Tajdid al-Siyasi wa al-Waqi' al-Arabi: Ru'iyah Islamiyah*, [Political Renewal and Arab Reality ; An Islamic Perspective] (Cairo: Markaz al Buhuth wa al-Dirasat al-Siyasiyah bi-Jama'at al-Qahirah,1989), pp.135-216

15. Abul-Fadl, *Madkhal Minhaji li-Dirasat al-Nuzum al-Siyasiyah al-Arabiyah*, op.cit., ppp.38-69

16. Ahmad Yusuf Ahmad, *al-Sira'at al-Arabiyah—al-Arabiyah: Bahth Istitla'i* [Arab-Arab Conflicts 1945-1981: A pilot study] (Beirut: Markaz Dirasat al-Wihda al-Arabiyah, 1988), pp.216.

17. Abul-Fadl, *Madkhal Minhaji li-Dirasat al-Nuzum al-Siyasiyah al-Arabiyah*, op.cit., pp.1-5

18. Muhammad al-Saiyd Sa'id, *Mustaqbal al-nizam al-Arabi Ba'd Azmat al-Khalij*, [Future of Arab Order after the Gulf Crisis] (Kuwait: Aalam al-Ma'rifa, no., 158, Feb. 1992), pp.21-23

19. Ibid., pp. 23-26

20. Ibid., pp.26-27

21. Muhammad Fathi Uthman, *al-Hudud al-Islamiyah al-Biyzantiyah bina al-Ihtikak al-Harbi wa al-Itisal al-Hadari*, [Muslim Roman Borders between Military Friction and Civilizational Communication] (Cairo: al-Dar al-Kawmiyah, 1966), 3 volumes

22. Sa'id, op.cit., pp.27-31

23. Giyrum Ghiyth, *Aflatun:Jadaliyat al-Fasad wa al-Sira' al-Tabaqi, Jadaliyat al-Muthul wa al-Musharakah, Jadaliyat al-Islaah wa al-Huriyah wa al-Wahdah*, [Plato: Dialectics of Corruption and Class Struggle, Dialectics of Ideals and Participation, Dialectics of Reform, Freedom, and Unity] (Beirut: Lebanese University Publications, Philosophical and Social Studies Depatment, 1982), p.135.

24. Theodore M. Benditt, "*The Concept of Interest in Political Theory*" *Political Theory*, vol. 3, no. 3, August 1973 , p.245

25. Christine Swanton, "*The Concept of Interest* " *Political Theory*, vol. 8, no. 1, February 1980, p.84, and Benditt, op.cit. p.245

26. al-Izz Ibn Abdul-Salaam, *Qawa'id al-Ahkam fi Masalih al-Anam*, [Rules of Islamic Legal Provisions as Regards People's Interests], vol.1, Revised by: Taha Abdul-Rauf Saad, (Cairo: Maktabat al-Kuliyat al-Azhariyah, 1991), pp.5-14, and Hussin Hamid Hassaan, *Nazariyat al-Maslaha fi al-Fiqh al-Islami* [Interest Theory in Islamic Jurisprudence] (Cairo: Maktabat al-Mutanabbi, 1981), pp.4-5.

27. Sa'id, op.cit., p.279

28. Ahmad, *al-Sira'at al-Arabiyah—al-Arabiyah: Bahth Istitla'i*, op.cit., p.215

29. Ibid., p.216

30. Tirbin, op.cit., p.7

31. Ahmad, *al-Sira'at al-Arabiyah—al-Arabiyah: Bahth Istitla'i*, op.cit., p.217

32. Ibid. pp.39-40

Conclusion

The most important aspect of the conclusion of this study lies in its identification of a number of central issues that will need further thinking and research:

1. The approach of most Arab researchers, when dealing with western thinking, has been partial and without depth, whether they accepted the west or rejected it. Either way, they were unwilling to reach a holistic and radical vision of the episteme they researched. They were satisfied with partialities and superficialities and took ideological positions, using scientific jargon to produce either a complete rejection or complete adoption. Their conclusions were not due to profound analysis.

2. Contemporary social sciences are multifaceted and diverse. They are in a state of continuous revision. There is no way to impose an ideological transformation of the notions and theories contained within them. This is outside the realm of science and its method, which requires inspection, criticism, deconstruction, reconstruction, continuous renovation, and development. The ideological treatment by Arab researchers of these sciences led to an epistemological disruption of their continuous development and froze Arab sciences at a certain point in time with a single, limited vision.

3. The nature and philosophy of comparison theory demands that we identify both the similarities and differences between states, systems, and societies. This is the justification for comparison. This gives results validity, for difference is not an abnormal state that must be abolished but the inevitable result of varied historical and social settings. This also means that inoculation and interchangeable benefits are possible without losing one's identity because comparison necessarily enriches knowledge about the other and thereby expands understanding, coexistence, and cooperation between cultures, civilizations, societies, and states. By considering the presence of diversity and multiplicity as a natural state that should be preserved, we should maximize the potential of each to benefit from the experience of the other.

4.Conducting research in a different epistemic system from that of the researcher requires a set of controlling values. The first of these values is expressed in the effort to achieve a level of scientific honesty that rests on more than a mere notion of objectivity with its superficial limitations. Of key importance here is the need for justice as a profound guiding value which the researcher applies in all stages of his work. The strength of this commitment to achieving an impartial under-standing of an alternative social reality should stand as the essential measure of one's scientific honesty. It should lead to a sense of fairness that controls the methods of gathering data, doing analysis and interpretation, and articulating results and evaluations. Scientific honesty built on a respectful appreciation of the other serves to distance the researcher from forgery, partiality, and distorted bias to prove certain points, even on the unconscious level. It makes it possible for one to approach truth even with those who differ or those who may be seen as enemies.

The aim of scientific research is to search for truths and seek reason beyond bias or advantage.

Bibliography

Abdul Fadil, Mahmoud: *al-Tashkilat wa al-Takwinaat al-Tabaqiyah fi al-Watan al-Arabi: Dirasah Tahliliyah Liaham al-Taturat wa al-Itijahat Kilal al-Fatrah 1945-1985*, Beirut: Markaz Dirasat al-Wihda al-Arabiyah, 1988.

Abdul-Qadir, Ali: ed., *Itijahat Hadithah fi Ilm al-Siyasah*, Cairo: Markaz al Buhuth wa al-Dirasat al-Siyasiyah bi-Jama'at al-Qahirah, 1987.

Abul-Fadl, Mona: *al-Umah al-Qutub*, Cairo , 1982.

Abul-Fadl, Mona: *Madkhal Minhaji fi Dirasat al-Nuzum Al-Siyasiyah al-Arabiyah*, Cairo: Faculty of Economics and Political Sciences, 1982.

Ahmad, Ahmad Yusuf: *al-Sira'at al-Arabiyah—al-Arabiyah: Bahth Istitla'I*, Beirut: Markaz Dirasat al-Wihda al-Arabiyah, 1988.

al-'Imari, Ahmad Sawaylim: *al-Nuzum al-Siyasiyah al-Hadithah lil Duwal al-Arabiyah*, Cairo: Matabit al-Anglo al-Misriyyah, 1969.

al-'Attar, Fa'wad *al-Nuzum al- Siyasiyah wa al-Qanun al-Dissturi*, Cairo: Dar al-Nahdah al-Arabiyah, 1974.

al-Affandi, Ahmad Kamil: *al-Nozum al-Hukumiyah al-Muqaranah*, kuwait: Wakalat al-Matbuaat,1982.

al-Gamal, Maisa: *al-Nukhbah al-Siyasiyah fi Misr, Al-Mustaqbal Al-Arabi*, Issue, no. 166, December 1992.

al-Gamal, Maisa: *al-Nukhbah al-Siyasiyah fi Misr: Dirasat Halat li-Majliss al-Wizaraa*, Beirut: Markaz Dirasat al-Wihda al-Arabiyah, 1993.

al-Hassan, Hassan: *al-Anzimah al-Dissturiyyah fi Labnan wa Sa'ir al-Buldan al-'Arabiyah*, Beirut: Dar Beirut lil-Taba'ah wa al-Nashr, 1981.

al-Hirmasi, Abdul-Latiyf: *"al-Harakat al-Islamiyah fi al-Mgrib al-Arabi" Al-Mustaqbal al-`Arabi*, Issue no.,156, Feb. 1992.

al-Hirmasy, Muhammad Abdul-Baqy: *al-Mujtama' wa al-Dawlah fi al-Magrib al-Arabi*, Beirut: Markaz Dirasat al-Wihda al-Arabiyah, 1987.

al-Imari, Ahmad Waaylim: *Usul al-Nuzum al- Siyasiyah al-Muqaranah*, Cairo: al-Hay'ah al-Misriyyah al-Amah lil Kitab, 1976.

al-Issawi, Ibrahim: *Qiyass al-Tabai'yah Fi al-Watan al-Arabi*, Beirut: Markaz Dirasat al-Wihda al-Arabiyah, 1989.

al-Khatib, Muhammad Fath-Allah: *Dirasat fi al-Hukumat al-Muqaranah*, Cairo: Dar al-Nahdah al-'Arabiyah, 1966.

al-Munufi, Kamal: *Usul al-Nuzum al-Siyasiyah al-Muqaranah*, Kuwait: Sharikat al-Robai'an,1987.

al-Naku', Mahmud Mahammad: *Azmat al-Nukhbah fi al-alam al-Arabi*, Published1989.

al-Naqib, Khaldun Hassan: *al-Dawlah al-Tassalutiyah fi al-Mashriq al-Arabi al-Mu'asir: Dirasah Bina'iyyah Muqaranah*, Beirut: Markaz Dirasat al-Wihda al-Arabiyah, 1991.

al-Naqib, Khaldun Hassan: *al-Mujtama' wa al-Dawlah fi al-Khalij wa al-Jazirah al-'Arabiyah*, Beirut: Markaz Dirasat al-Wihda al-Arabiyah, 1987.

al-Naqib, Khaldun: *"Binaa' al-Mujtam' al-Arabi: Ba'd al-Furud al-Bahthiyah" Al-Mustaqbal al-'Arabi*, Issue no. 73, September 1985.

al-Rashiydi, Ahmad: ed., *al-Ina'kasat al-Dawliyah wa al-Iqliymiyah li-Azmat al-Khalij*, Cairo: Markaz al Buhuth wa al-Dirasat al-Siyasiyah bi-Jama'at al-Qahirah, 1991.

al-Sa'iyd, Ni'ma: *al-Nuzum al-Siyasiyah fi al-Sharq al-Awsat*, Baghdad: Sharkat al-Tab' wa al-Nashr al-Ahliyyah, 1968.

al-Saiyd, Mustafa Kamil: ed., *Hatah la Tansha' Harb Arabiyah-Arabiyah Ukhra: Min Duruss Harb al-Khalij*, Cairo: Markaz al Buhuth wa al-Dirasat al-Siyasiyah bi-Jama'at al-Qahirah, 1991.

al-Samrai', Manal Yunus: *al-Mar'ah wa al- Tatwur al-Siyasi fi al-Watan alArabi*, MA Thesis, Institute of Arab Research and Studies,1988.

al-Sayid, Mustafa Kamil: ed., *al-Tahawlat al-Siyasiyah al-Hadithah fi al-Watan al-Arabi*, Cairo: Markaz al Buhuth wa al-Dirasat al-Siyasiyah bi-Jama'at al-Qahirah, 1989.

al-Zaahiry, Mohammed Hassan: *al-Dawur al-Siyasi lil-Qabilah fi al-Yaman 1962-1990*, Cairo: Madbuly Library, 1996.

Anssari, Hamid: *"Hudood al-Sultah al-Khassah bil-Nukhabal-Hakimah: al-Tama'tu' bi-Sultah Datiyyah fi Manzur Muqaran" Al-Mustaqbal al-'Arabi*, Issue no.,113, July 1988.

Aref, Mohammed: *al-Manhag fi Ilm al-Igtemaa'* Cairo: Dar al-Thakafa, 1972.

'Arif, Nasr Muhammad: *fi Musadir al-Turath al-Siyasi al-Islami: Dirasah fi Ishkaliyat al-Ta'mim qabl al-Istiqra' wa al-Ta'sil*, Herndon VA: al-Ma'had al-Alamiyyah li'l-Fikr al-Islami, 1994.

Arif, Nasr: *The Re-enchantment of Political Scienc:Theories of Comparative Politics, An Epistemological Approach*, (Binghamton:State University of New York Press, Forthcoming)

'Asaf, 'Abd al-Mu'ti Muhammad: *"Azmat al-Fa'aliyah al-Siyasiyah fi al-Bilaad al-Arabiyah: Itar nazari Muqaran," Al-Mustaqbal al-'Arabi*, Issue no.,36, Feb 1982, Republished in: *Sha'un 'Arabiyah*, Issue no., 12, Feb, 1982.

Badran, Wadudah: ed., *Iqtirabat al-Ba'hth fi al-'ulum al-Ijtima'iyah*, Cairo: Markaz al-Bahuth wa al-Dirasat al-Siyasiyyah bi-Jami'at al-Qahirah, 1992.

Barakat, Halim: *al-Mujtam' al-'Arabi al-Mu'asir*, Beirut: Markaz Dirasat al-Wihda al-Arabiyah, 1986.

Bel'id, al-Sadiq: *"Door al-Mu'assassat al-Deniyah fi Da'm al-Anzimah al-Siyasiyah fi al-Bilaad al-Arabiyah" Al-Mustaqbal al-`Arabi*, Issue no.,108, feb 1988.

Benditt, Theodore M.: *"The Concept of Interest in Political Theory " Political Theory*, vol. 3, no. 3, August 1973.

Bill, James: and. Hardgrave, Robert L.: *Comparative Politics: The Quest for Theory. Columbus*, Ohio: Charles E. Merrill, 1973.

Bottomore, T.B.: *Elites and Society*, New York: Basic Books, 1964.

Cantori, Louis: and Andrew Ziegler Jr., eds., *Comparative Politics in the Post-Behavioral Era*, Boulder, CO: Lynne Rienner Publishers,1988.

Chilcote, Ronald: *Theories of Comparative Politics*, Boulder, CO: Westview Press,1981.

Davis, John: *Libyan Politics: Trib and Revolution*, London: Tours andCo.LIT,1987.

Dawud, Muhammad Suliyman: *Nazariyat al-Qiyas al-Usuli Manhaj Tajriybi Islami: Drasah Muqaranah*, Alexandria: Dar al-Dawah, 1984.

Dessouki,`Ali E. Hillal: *Madkhal fi al-Nozum al-Siyasiyah al-Muqaranah*, Cairo: Faculty of Economics and Political Sciences, 1975.

Deutsch, Karl: *Politics and Government: How People Decide Their Fate*, Boston: Houghton Mifflin 1974.

Eppel, Michael: *"The Elite,The Effendiyya,and the growth of Nationalism and Pan-Arabism in Hashemite Iraq,1921-1958," International Journal of Middle East Studies*,vol.30,no.2,May1998.

Fahmi, Mustafa Abu Zayd: *Mabadi' al-Nuzum al- Siyasiyah*, Alexandria: Monsha't al-Ma'rif, 1984.

Field, G. Lowell: Comparative Political Development: The Precedent of the West, New York: Cornell University Press, 1967.

Ghaliyun, Burhan: *al-Mihnah al-Arabiyah: al-Dawlah Did al-Umah*, Beirut: Markaz Dirasat al-Wihda al-Arabiyah, 1993.

Ghanim, Al-Sayid 'Abd al-Mutalib: *al-Itijahat al-Mu'sirah fi Dirasat al-Nuzum al-Siyasiyah*, Cairo: Dar al-Qahirah lil-Nashr wa al-Tawzi', 1985.

Ghiyth, Giyrum: *Aflatun:Jadaliyat al-Fasad wa al-Sira' al-Tabaqi, Jadaliyat al-Muthul wa al-Musharakah, Jadaliyat al-Islaah wa al-Huriyah wa al-Wahdah*, Beirut: Lebanese University Publications, Philosophical and Social Studies Depatment, 1982.

Hague, Rod: and Harrop, Martin: *Comparative Government and Politics: An Introduction*,London: Macmillan Education, 1987.

Hammergren, Lim A.: *"Corporatism in Latin American Politics: a Reexamination of the Unique Tradition," Comparative Politics*, vol.9, no.4 July,1977.

Harik, Ilya: *"al-Dawlah al-Ra'wiyah wa Mustqbal al-Tanmiyah al-Arabiyah" Al-Mustaqbal al-`Arabi*, Issue no.,121, March 1989.

Harik, Ilya: *"Nushu' Nizam al-Dawlah fi al-Watan al-Arabi," Al-Mustaqbal al-`Arabi*, Issue no., 99, May 1987.

Hariq, Iliya: *"al-Suratiyah wa al-Tahuwil al-Siyasi fi al-Mujtam` al-Arabi," Al-Mustaqbal al-`Arabi*, Issue no. 80, October 1985.

Hassaan, Hussin Hamid: *Nazariyat al-Maslaha fi al-Fiqh al-Islami*, Cairo: Maktabat al-Mutanabbi, 1981.

Ibn Abdul-Salaam, al-Izz: *Qawa'id al-Ahkam fi Masalih al-Anam*, Revised by: Taha Abdul-Rauf Saad, Cairo: Maktabat al-Kuliyat al-Azhariyah, 1991.

Ibn-Khaldun. *Muqaddemat Ibn-Khaldun*, Beirut: al-Aalamy Publications.

Ibn-Manzour : *Lessan al-Arab*, Cairo, Dar al-Maarif, 1979.

Ibrahim, Hassanian Tawfiq: *Dhahiyrat al-Unif al-Siyasi fi al-Nuzum al-Arabiyah*, Ph.D. Cairo University,1990.

Ibrahim, Sa'd el-Din: *"Masadir al-Shari'yah fi AnzimaT al-Hukm al-'Arabiyah,"* *Al-Mustaqbal al-'Arabi*, Issue no., 62, April 1984.

Ibrahim, Sa'd el-Din: *al-Mujtama' wa al-Dawlah fi al-Watan al-Arabi*, Beirut: Markaz Dirasat al-Wihda al-Arabiyah, 1988.

Imam, Samia Said: *al-usul al-Ijtima'iyah li- Nukhbat al-Infitaah fi Misr 1974-1980*, MA. Thesis, Cairo University 1988.

Ismai'l, Saif al-Deen: *al-Tajdid al-Siyasi wa al-Waqi' al-Arabi: Ru'iyah Islamiyah*, Cairo: Markaz al Buhuth wa al-Dirasat al-Siyasiyah bi-Jama'at al-Qahirah,1989.

Kaylali, F.: and Kufalzun, M.: *al-Madiyah al-Tarikhiyah*, , translated from Russian to Arabic by Ahmad Dawud, Damascus: dar al-Jamahir, 1970.

Khalil, Muhsin: *al-Nuzum al-Siyasiyah wa al-Qanun al-Dissturi*,Alexandria: Monsha't al-Ma'rif, 1971.

Kharbush, Muhammad Safi-Udin: *al-Fikr al-Qawmi wa al-Siyasah al-Arabiyah ma' al-Tatbiyq ala Misr wa Soriyah wa al-Jaza'ir*, Ph.D. Cairo University, 1989.

Kharbush, Muhammad Safi-Udin: *al-Mutagiyer al –Tanzimi fi Binaa al-Sultah fi al-Watan al-Arabi*, MA Thesis. Cairo University, 1986.

Khoury, Philip S.: and Kostiner, Joseph: *Tribes and State Formation in the Middle East*, Berkeley: University of California Press, 1990.

Laylah, Muhammad Kamil: *al-Nuzum al-Siyasiyah: al-Dawlah wa al-Hukumah*,Cairo: Dar al-Fikr al-Arabi, 1967.

Leacock, Stephen: *Elements of Political Science*, Boston and New York: Houghton Mifflin Company, 1906.

Lenczowski, George: ed., *Political Elite in the Middle East*, Washington DC: American Enterprise Institute for Public Research,1975.

Marger, Martin N.: *Elites and Masses: An Introduction to Political Sociology*, New York: Van Nostrand, 1991.

Massarah, Intwan Nasri: *"Tanziym al-Ilaqah biyna al-Din wa al-Siyasah fi al-Anzimah al-Arabiyah al-Mu'asirah: Bahth fi Nazariyah Amah Istinadan ila Halati Lybnan wa Misr" Al-Mustaqbal al-'Arabi*, Issue no.131, Jan. 1990.

Mayer Lawrence C.: *"Practicing What We Preach: Comparative Politics in the 1980s," Comparative Political Studies*, vol.16, no.2 July 1983.

Merrit, Richard L.: and Rokkan, Stein: eds., *Comparing Nations: The Use of Quantitative Data in Cross-National Research*, London: Yale University Press,1986.

Merritt, Richard L.: *Systematic Approach to Comparative Politics*, Chicago: Rand McNally, 1971.

Mitkeis, Hoda Hafez: *al-Nukhbah al-Siyasiyah fi Tunis, 1956-1970*, M.A. thesis, Cairo University, 1981.

Mua'wad, Jalal: *Alaqat al-Qiyyada bil-Dhahiyrah al-Inma'iyah: Dirassah fi al-Mantiqah al-Arabiyah*, Ph.D. Cairo University, 1985.

Muhammad, Hassani: *al-Sulutat al-Istisna'iyah li-Ra'iys al-Dawlah fi al-Nizam al-Ri'assi: Dirasah Muqaranah lil Wilaiyat al-Mutahidah wa Misr wa al-Iraaq wa al-Jaza'ir*MA Thesis, Institute of Arab Research and Studies,1985.

Musa'd, Neven: *al-Aqliyat wa al-Istiqrar al-siyasi fi al-Watan al-Arabi*, Ph.D. Cairo University, 1987.

Musa'd, Neven: ed., *al-Aalamiyah wa al-Khussusiyah fi Dirasat al Mantiqah al-Arabiyah*, Cairo: Markaz al Buhuth wa al-Dirasat al-Siyasiyah bi-Jama'at al-Qahirah, 1991.

Musa'd, Neven: ed., *al-Tahawlat al-Demucratiyah fi al-Watan al-Arabi*, Cairo: Markaz al Buhuth wa al-Dirasat al-Siyasiyah bi-Jama'at al-Qahirah, 1993.

Mutawwali, 'Abd al-Hamid: *al-Anzimah al-Siyasiyah wa al-Mabadi' al-Distoriyah al-Aamah*, Cairo: Dar al-Ma'arif,1957.

Nadwat al-Mujtam' al-Madani fi al-Watan al-Arabi wa durahu fi Tahqiq al-Demcratiyah, Beirut: Markaz Dirasat al-Wihda al-Arabiyah, 1992.

Nadwat al-Ulum al-Siyasiyah fi al-Watan al-Arabi, Cyprus: Arab Association of Political Sciences, February 4-8, 1985.

Nadwat Azmat al-demucratiyah fi al-Watan al-Arabi, Beirut: Markaz Dirasat al-Wihda al-Arabiyah, 1984.

Nadwat Manahij al-Tagiyr fi al-Fikr al-Islami, Ministry of Awqaf, Kuwait , 24-26th Jan. 1994.

Niessen, Manfred: and Peschar, Jules: eds., *International Comparative Research: Problems and Methodology, Methodology and Organization in Eastern Europe*, Oxford: Pergamon Press,1982.

Nye, Robert A.: *The Anti-democratic Source of Elite Theory: Pareto, Mosca and Michels*, London: Sage Publications, 1977.

'Obidan, Yusaf Muhammad: *Nizam al-Hukm fi Duwal al-Khalij: Dirasah Muqaranah li Qatar, al-Kuwait wa al-Bahrain*, Ph.D. Cairo University,1 982.

Oyen, Else: *"The Imperfections of Comparisons"* in Else Oyen, ed., *Comparative Methodology: Theory and Practice in International Social Research* (London: Sage Publication, 1990.

Pappe, Ilan: and Ma'oz, Moshe: *Middle Eastern Politics and Ideas: A History From Within*, London: Touris Academic Studies,1997.

Popper, Karl: *The Logic of Scientific Discovery*, New York: Science Editions, 1961.

Rabai', Hamid: *al-Thaqafa al-Arabiyah bina al-Gazwu al-Sihuni wa Iradat al-Takamul al-qawmi*, Cairo: Dar al-Mawkif al-Arabi, 1983.

Rida, Muhammad Jawaad: *Sira' al-Dawlah wa al-Kabilah fi al-Khlij al-Arabi: Azamaat al-Tnmiyah wa Tanmiyat al-Azamaat*, Beirut: Markaz Dirasat al-Wihda al-Arabiyah, 1992.

Sa'id, Muhammad al-Saiyd: *Mustaqbal al-nizam al-Arabi Ba'd Azmat al-Khalij,* Kuwait, Aalam al-Ma'rifa, no., 158, Feb. 1992.

Sa'iyd, Abdul Mun'im: ed., *Tadris al-'Ulum al-siyasiyah fi al-Watan al-'Arabi,* Cairo: Markaz al Buhuth wa al-Dirasat al-Siyasiyah bi-Jama'at al-Qahirah, 1990.

Salamah, Gassan: *"Quwat al-Dawlah wa Da'fihaa: Bahth fi al-Thakafa al-Siyasiyah al-Arabiyah," Al-Mustaqbal al-'Arabi,* Issue no., 99, May 1987.

Salih, 'Ata Muhammad: and Taym, Fawzi Ahmad: *al-Nuzum al-Siyasiyah al-'Arabiyah al-Mu'asirah,* Benghazi: Manshurat Jami'at Qaryuns, 1988.

Sari, Salim: *"al-Ijtima'iyun al-'Arab wa Dirasat al-Qadaya al-Mujtama'iyah al-'Arabiyah: Mumarasah Naqdiyah," al-Mustaqbal al-'Arabi,* issue 75, May 1985.

Sartori, Giovanni: *"Concept Misformation in Comparative Politics," The American Political Science Review,* vol. 64, no. 4, December 1970.

Sha'ban, al-Sadiq: *"al-Huquq al-Siyasiyah lil al-Insan fi al-dassateer al-Arabiyah" Al-Mustaqbal al-'Arabi,* Issue no.106, December 1987.

Shafiq, Munir: *al-Islam wa Tahadiyat al-Inhitat al-Mu'asr: Qadaiya al-Tajziyah, wa al-Suhuniyah, wa al-Tagtiyb,* Cairo: al-Zahraa lil-I'lam al-Arabi, 1987.

Shari'ati, Ali: *al-Awoda ila al-dhat,* translated from Persian to Arabic by Ibrahim Shiyta, Cairo: al-dhahraa lil I'lam al-Arabi 1986.

Sirhal, Ahmad: *al-nuzum al-Siyasiyah wa al-Dissturiyah fi Labnan wa Kafat al-Dewal al-'Arabiyah,* Beirut: Dar al-Fikr al-Arabi, 1990.

Swanton, Christine: *"The Concept of Interest " Political Theory,* vol. 8, no. 1, February 1980.

Thabit, Ahmad: *"al-Ta'adudiyah al-Siyasiyah fi al-Watan al-Arabi," Al-Mustaqbal al-'Arabi,* Issue no.155, Jan. 1992.

The Qura'n,

Tirbin, Ahmad: *al-Tajzi'ah al-Arabiyah: Kaiyfa Hadathat Tariykhiyan?,* Beirut: Markaz Dirasat al-Wihda al-Arabiyah, 1987.

Uthman, Muhammad Fathi: *al-Hudud al-Islamiyah al-Biyzantiyah bina al-Ihtikak al-Harbi wa al-Itisal al-Hadari,* Cairo: al-Dar al-Kawmiyah, 1966.

White, Stephen: Gardner, Johon: Schopflin, Georg: and Saich, Tony: *Communist and Postcommunist Political Systems: An Introduction,* New York: St. Martin's Press, 1990.

Wiarda, Haward: ed., *New Directions in Comparative Politics.* Boulder, CO: Westview Press, 1991.

Zaiyn al-Abidiyn, al-Tayyb: ed., *al-Manhaageyah al-Islamiyyah wa al-Uloom al-Slookiyah wa al-Tarbawiyah,* Hendon,VA: International Institute of Islamic Thought , 1990.

Zannoni, Paolo: *"The Concept of Elite," European Journal of Political Research,* vol. 6, 1978.

Zarnooqah, Salah Salim: *Anmaat Intiqal al-Sultah fi al-Bilaad al-Arabiyah1949-1985,* MA Thesis, Cairo University, 1989.

Zarnooqah, Salah Salim: *Anmat Intiqal al-Sultah fi al-Nuzum al-Wirathiyah al-Arabiyah1950-1985, Al-Mustaqbal al-'Arabi,* Issue no., 140, October 1990.

Zuhran,Jamal 'Ali: *Manahij Qiyas Quwat al-Dawlah ma' al-Tatbiyq ala Tawazun al-Quwah bina al-Arab wa Isra'iyl*, Ph.D. Cairo university,1988.

Index

Abul-Fadl   33, 36
Africa   62
al-Fadil   25-28, 30
al-Gabri   25, 26
Algeria   12, 76
al-Ghazali   86
al-Sayid   28, 29, 31
Arab League   7, 13, 84, 85
Arab nationalism   11
Arab solidarity   88
Asian   27, 29, 62
authoritarianism   43
Awqaf   26

Barakat   14
Bedouin   25, 26
behaviorism   vii, 5, 6, 9, 11, 12, 43, 56,
Bottomore   57, 58
bureaucratic   10, 66

Cairo University   1, 4-8, 13, 15
Cantori   39
capitalism   29, 31, 65, 66
Christianity   49
civil society   28, 44
civilizational perspective   32, 34-36
class analysis   viii, 2, 3, 6, 10, 11, 24,
      26, 28, 31, 32, 41, 56
constitution   5, 6, 10, 41, 63
corporatism   vii, 42, 66

decision-making approach   2, 65

democracy   43
dependency theory   36
description   5, 9, 11, 12, 14, 80
Deutsch   36, 58
dialectic materialism   30, 31
dynasty   51, 61

Easton   2, 36, 41, 65
Egypt   4, 12, 14, 25, 26, 44, 50, 51,
      63, 65, 66, 75, 76, 84, 89
election   41
elite theory   6, 11, 24, 55-58, 60-66
empirical   3, 7, 8, 10, 12, 28, 30, 31,
      44, 89
epistemology   28, 48
ethnicity   60, 63, 74, 85
ethnocentrism   28
Eurocentrism   44
Europe   5, 27-30, 34, 44, 51, 75, 76,
      85

feudalism   27

Germany   48, 74
Ghalion   47
Ghanim   3
governance   55, 82
Gulf states   63

Hegelian   44
hegemony   4, 29
heritage   28, 33, 49, 51, 61, 62

historical materialism   27, 28, 30, 31, 35

Ibn Khaldun   25-27
ideological   viii, 3, 11, 13, 15, 23, 24, 26, 28, 30, 32, 34, 44-46, 51, 86, 93
independence   28, 56, 76, 83, 84
institutional analysis   5, 10
institution   41, 50, 77, 85
intellectual   49, 50, 59, 60, 67, 73, 78, 80-82
interest groups   5, 7, 41, 42
Iran   73
Iraq   12, 31, 63, 75, 76, 83, 84
Islam   4, 35, 48, 74, 80, 81, 85
Islamic movement   87
Ismail Pasha   51

knowledge   2, 12, 32, 34, 40, 44, 50, 71, 79, 82, 93

Lassewell   41
Latin American   43
Layla   3
Leacock   4
legal school   5
legitimacy   12, 33-35, 47, 63, 64, 73, 75-77, 82, 83, 87

majority   3, 57
Marxism   vii, 24, 28-31, 34
Michels   58, 59
military   25, 26, 48, 58, 59, 63, 64, 74, 81
minority   3, 26, 57, 58, 60
modernity   11, 33, 44, 80
Mosca   58, 59

nation-state   48, 74, 75, 85, 86

oligarchy   58, 59
Ottoman empire   76, 85

Pan Arabism   87
paradigm   33, 34, 39, 40, 42, 43, 46, 49, 50, 51
Pareto   58, 59
party   63, 72, 80, 83
patron-client relationship   63, 64
Persian   84
Plato   85
pluralism   57
political class   58
political economy   vii, 42, 65, 66
post-behaviorism   vii, 43
post-modernism   43, 44
prescription   15
primitive society   59
proletariat   31
public opinion   41, 57, 82

qualitative   30, 44
quantitative   10, 30, 44, 45

Raymond   26
reconciliation   v, 71-73, 76-78, 85, 87-89
reform   61, 72, 73, 77-79, 83, 85, 87
religion   25, 26, 34, 49, 56, 58, 60, 63, 79,
revelation   34
Roman civilization   49

Saudi Arabia   63, 75, 84
Schimtter   66
So'udi   1-3
Springburg   64
stability   41, 59, 61, 63, 74, 83
state-society relation   vii, 42, 55, 64
structural-functional   vii, 2, 3, 6, 10, 11, 36, 56
structuralism   10
Sudan   12, 76, 89
Syria   12, 44, 63, 75, 76

third world   27, 29, 31, 43

totalitarianism   43
traditional methods   10
traditionalism   12, 56
transitional state   43
tribalism   80, 85
Turkey   73

Weberian-Parsonian   24
westernization   50
Wiarda   43

Yemen   12, 63, 84

Zaghal   27